Comeback Moms

MONICA SAMUELS
and J. C. CONKLIN

Comeback Moms

*How to Leave Work,
Raise Children, and
Restart Your Career
Even If You Haven't
Worked in Years*

MORGAN ROAD BOOKS
New York

MORGAN ROAD BOOKS

Published by Morgan Road Books, an imprint of The Doubleday Broadway Publishing Group, a division of Random House, Inc.

PRINTED IN THE UNITED STATES OF AMERICA

Morgan Road Books and the M colophon are trademarks of Random House, Inc.

Visit our Web site at www.morganroadbooks.com

Book design by Nicola Ferguson

Cataloging-in-Publication Data is on file with the Library of Congress.

ISBN 0-7679-2242-5

10 9 8 7 6 5 4 3 2 1

First Edition

This book is dedicated to our mothers,
June Leiter and Linda Hale Conklin

Acknowledgments

Without these people and their patience and graciousness, we wouldn't have a book: Helen Mobley, Dr. Dave Streicher, Suzanne Standerfer, Sara Fox, Dee Dee Benkie, Kelly McBrayer, Dr. JoAnn McMillan, Ann Howard, Anne Heiligenstein, Michael Mack, The Wednesday Morning Group, Robin Gilchrist, Sonia Medina, Craig Beskid, Judy Potter, Bill Miller, our agent, Kathleen Anderson, and the editors and staff at Morgan Books: Amy Hertz, Marc Haeringer, and Nate Brown.

We'd also like to thank our families: Marc, Jared, Chase, Larry Leiter, Lisa Morris, Dana Corbett, Stanley Farrer, Dr. Elizabete Santos, Dr. Jeremy Conklin, Dr. Richard Conklin, Dr. Jan Conklin, C. J. Hernandez, and Kimble Ross.

Contents

Introduction

ARE YOU TOAST?

We're undergoing a sea change in this country—millions of women are quitting their jobs to stay home and raise their children.

That would never be you, right? That's what we thought and boy, were we wrong. Hear us out. Once you have a baby, your life changes in ways you'd never imagine. We don't just mean hallucinating and talking to yourself after several months of sleep deprivation. You have no idea how much you'll love that little baby. It makes you a little crazy—crazy enough to leave a six-figure salary and paid vacations to stay home with said baby.

Before you storm into your boss's office and tell her she won't be seeing you around anymore, read this book. There's more to quitting than saying the words. There's strategy involved.

Think about it. You're most likely cutting your household income in half, sending yourself on an extended time-out from adult contact, and putting your ego in a piñata that some patronizing people will whack at will: "How can you stand to be home with your children all day? So why did you even become a lawyer/doctor/teacher?" Not to mention that in a few years you'll probably want to go back to work and, without laying some groundwork now, your choices aren't gonna be pretty later. It's not easy out there even when you don't take time off.

Trust us, Monica and the women we talked to for this book are doing what you're contemplating. We know what we're talking about. True, we don't have all the answers—but we have a lot of experience and we've stockpiled stories of epic errors that we don't want you to make.

This book is for women who think they might have children someday, are bent over with morning sickness all day, have a little baby in day care, have another child on the way, or might have a child if their husband really, really wants one someday. In short, it's for every woman of childbearing age, and their mothers too because, well, your mom can tell you what we left out.

The reality is we women compete in the workplace with men who, although they may be great fathers, aren't mothers—and there's a whole lot more work to do as a mother. Mothers typically are the ones managing child-care arrangements, staying home with sick children, and convulsing with guilt when they miss a soccer game. They are also, by large numbers—we're talking millions—the parent who opts to stay home with the children. What this means is that women who take time off are competing with men who don't. Is that an equal playing field? Does changing diapers for two years spell career advancement?

If you take a couple years off to raise your children is your career toast?

One boss we talked to laughed when we asked him that question and said we should title the book *Hopeless*, because that's exactly what the woman wanting to get back into the workforce after time off will be.

He's right. Let us modify that: he's right for some women. Those who give up easily, like at the first sign of failure, aren't going to make it. Those who take no for an answer won't get farther than the first closed door. Those who don't plan for their future won't have more than the next day to look forward to.

If you do it right you can reposition yourself professionally, perhaps becoming something you never thought possible. You can get back on the same track, shift gears, accelerate, make sharp turns, or change careers entirely. You can start your own business.

The time you take off to spend with your kids and away from the jobsite could not only be the most gratifying personal decision you could make, it might also be the best professional move you could make, if you look at it a little farther downstream. It's all about the planning. This book is your time machine. You can fast forward and see your future through the eyes of those women who have been there and done that.

Let us show you how to strategize step by step how to leave the office so that you'll be able to come back, or if you've been gone for a while, we can show you how to get back into a successful second career.

We know women who have done it. It is possible. You have to learn how to keep your hand in the game. Keeping your hand in can mean taking on all sorts of activities including volunteering to help the cultural exchange program at your son's school, becoming active in local politics, or becoming so frustrated at your child's artistic tendencies with mashed potatoes and carrots in restaurants that you create a device that will clean up his mess easier.

WHY WE WROTE THIS BOOK

Monica's Story

It happened as I was standing in front of the salad bar at the Radisson Hotel restaurant in Orlando, Florida. When the smell of slightly curdled bleu cheese dressing was making me sick, I knew I couldn't go back to work.

I was two months pregnant for the second time and working on a presidential campaign. If my candidate won, I'd win a brag-worthy job. It would be the culmination of all the hundreds of meetings I attended. And I couldn't do it.

Up until that very moment, I appeared to be at the top of my game. Years earlier, amid a legal career and motherhood, my lifelong love of politics became more than a passing interest. The Young Republican National Federation elected me their national chairwoman. That event introduced me to a world of elected officials, party leaders, and political operatives. Among the latter group was Karl Rove, who kindly invited me to join the 2000 Bush presidential campaign as a paid staffer. While working on the campaign in the final weeks, I found myself in this hotel standing in front of rubbery hard-boiled eggs ready to retch.

Weeks before, my husband and I received the news that I was pregnant. While in most circles this is joyous news, it is not the sort of thing that one shares around the watercooler with the rest of the political team who are all working 24/7 and eating cold pizza until (they hope) Election Day. Consequently, I kept the news to myself.

So there I was in Orlando, where the Coalitions Team sent me three weeks before the election to try to organize and mobilize young voters, gripped by morning sickness (which in my case lasted all day) and thus barely able to mobilize myself, much less anyone else.

Slowly, I lifted the plastic salad bar tongs and tried to select something that looked halfway edible to a woman whose hormones were in the spin cycle. As I picked through the olives, carrots, and sliced cucumbers, waves of nausea and lightheadedness flooded over me. Soon the only thing I could smell were leaves. Yuck. Leaves. No way could I eat leaves in this condition. I searched desperately for anything to keep me going. Finally, I spotted it. The answer to my prayers . . . saltine crackers. Carefully, I removed a bag of crackers from the basket and, feeling faint, slowly walked to my assigned table in the restaurant.

Taking my seat, I opened the bag and bit into the first of two crackers. Sitting there, I slowly chewed the saltine like a centurion whose dentures were missing, contemplated my life, and reached a conclusion. Despite what I continually tried to tell myself, I really didn't have it all together.

As I sat there it dawned on me, *At this very moment, while I'm dining alone and contemplating a trip later in the day to the nearest emergency room, our nanny is home with my four-year-old son, feeding and dressing him, hearing about his day, and comforting him at night when his newly acquired fear of the dark kicks in at bedtime.*

Despite my eagerness to conquer the world, it occurred to me that I really was failing at the one thing I regarded as the most important role I had—being my son's mom. With another child on the way, I realized that if I continued down my current path, I would risk simply try-ing to fit yet another person into my crowded and busy life rather than having a deep meaningful relationship with someone who should be of utmost importance to me—my child. I made a decision.

No matter what happens in this election, I thought, my next job will be full-time mom.

Coming to this conclusion wasn't easy. Few people ever get the chance to work on a presidential campaign. For the staffers of a successful campaign, the victor's move to residence at 1600 Pennsylvania Avenue comes with exciting job opportunities for many of those hardy souls who toiled to get him there. Making this decision meant giving up a chance to move up the career ladder while doing something truly exciting that I loved. More important, though, it meant coming to grips with reality. I simply couldn't do everything well, so I finally needed to choose.

As things were, if everything went perfectly, I could be at best a pretty good attorney and a pretty good mom. Since things are rarely ever perfect, achieving a rating of "pretty good" probably wasn't likely on either score. I really couldn't be great at either job. Between the two op-tions, I concluded that motherhood meant more to me, and I'm glad I did.

J.C.'s Story

I'm not a mother yet. I want to be one, but the truth is it scares the hell out of me. I see working mothers who would kill for six straight hours of sleep. I talk to stay-at-home mothers who mourn the loss of their careers because they were so intertwined with their work that it defined who they were. The loss of their jobs stripped them of their sense of self. The loss frequently resulted in resentment, compromising the very thing for which they had sacrificed. I talk to working mothers who struggle with the guilt of missing events in their children's lives. I remember my own mother slipping into the back of the auditorium well after the school play had started, hoping no one would notice.

Even from my vicarious distance, I understand it's hard. I also know from painful, firsthand experience that women are sometimes the harshest critics of other women. I have talked to working mothers who said they would never hire another working mother because they know her loyalties would be split between her job and her children. Other women have told me that they were so worried about appearing weak to their colleagues and supervisors that days after giving birth they were back on conference calls. One even held a meeting in her living room while she breastfed her four-day-old infant.

I know there must be a better balance than what I've seen. There must be a way to raise your kids and have a career. That's why I wanted to write this book. I wanted to find out what the pioneers of this movement have experienced. By pioneers, I mean the women who have figured out a way to do this without going insane. Pioneers are the women who will change what it's like for all of us to be mothers. After hundreds of hours of conversations and interviews, a pattern, even a philosophy, seems to have emerged from their struggles. These women started out trying to do it all and found if they continued that path they'd go insane. They gave themselves permission to put candles on a storebought birthday cake for their children. They stopped marking professional accomplishments on a precise mental calendar. They came to terms with a pile of dirty dishes in the sink and a vacuum cleaner that is rarely turned on. One woman said to me when I asked how she managed her children and career, "I don't. If I have a good day at work, I have a not so good day with my kids and vice versa. I accept that when I go to bed at night I don't feel a hundred percent about one part of my life." I've nicknamed the phenomenon the seesaw effect: women's lives will dip back and forth between work and home. We won't feel a hundred percent about either of them at the same time, but that's okay.

To me, these women are the new women's liberationists. They're saying we don't have to work like men to be successful. We can do this on our own terms, and truth be told, I've talked to several men who are envious of what women have invented and to other women who are angry with them for doing it. Their cumulative experiences have given me hope that motherhood and career are not mutually exclusive, that there's more out there than stress and sleep deprivation. There's opportunity to become something else, something new—a mother who knows she doesn't have to do it all, all at once.

Comeback
Moms

1
Quitting

When Is the Best Time to Cut the Cord?

Maybe you just got the news that you're expecting or maybe you're a veteran mom with middle school–aged kids at home, it doesn't matter where you are on the mom continuum, at some point you'll be confronted with the burning question: Should you stay home with your children? Should you leave a job you love to stay home with your children who you love?

That question avalanches into a blizzard of other worries. If you quit to assume this new role at home, will your career be over? Will you ever work again and if you do will it be in a job you find fulfilling or will it be in a position for which you'll memorize three words: "paper or plastic?"

You stay up late with your friends and debate whether or not you can have it all—career and family. And, like a lot of us, you find that you can't. At least not all at once.

SUBVERTING THE GUILT PARADIGM

There are basically two reasons mothers decide to quit their jobs—guilt and love.

We visit the day-care facilities we'll be leaving our newborns in. We see row upon row of cribs decorated with a few items from home—sort of the way inmates adorn their prison cells. We see the babies sleeping or staring at the ceiling but not doing much else until their number comes up for a diaper change or bottle.

We see this and we think—not our babies. We're not going to do that to our babies. So we quit to diaper and feed them ourselves.

Or we tough it out for a few years and one day we catch ourselves staring at our computer screens thinking, *What am I doing here at www.anythingtolookbusy.com while my children see me just a couple of hours each evening and on weekends?* This isn't worth it. So we quit.

WAIT! WHY DO YOU *REALLY* WANT TO STAY HOME?

This may seem obvious. You want to quit because you want to nurture your baby. Just like we said, right? You want to watch your child learn to crawl and walk. But, before you even think about quitting, let's make sure that's what's going on.

Our friend, Darcy, is a good example of why not to quit your job.

Darcy didn't just hate her job, she loathed being a physical therapist. She moved from office to office until she ran out of places to go and she realized it wasn't the people, it was the work;

she abhorred the tedious insurance forms. Because she hated her job, her husband and two children were miserable. Nobody wanted to be within one hundred feet of Mommy when she returned from work each day for fear of finding out that once again she had a bad day at the office.

At lunch one day, we noticed Darcy wasn't her normal tense self. She told us that she and her husband were considering her quitting her job to stay home with their kids.

"We know it will be tough," Darcy explained between bites of Caesar salad, "but we think it's the right thing to do."

Two months later, Darcy made the big move. Rather than leave quietly, she made sure that all the other therapists knew that she hated the place and was glad to be going. Her departing remark was something along the lines of, "Good luck, suckers."

A week after her departure, we lunched while her kids were in school. She was happy and full of plans.

"We definitely need to do a spa day," she told us excitedly. "And maybe we could all get together for drinks one night a week. I'm also thinking a girls' trip to Hawaii might be nice."

We looked across the table at each other, and it was clear we were both thinking the same thing. Alarm bells were sounding over Darcy's head.

She thinks she's on vacation!

A month later she shared her itinerary with us. The children were out of school for the summer, so she had lots of time to spend with them. Darcy said she had taken the children shopping, swimming, golfing, and to some of the better restaurants in town. She had also seen almost every movie playing. Her elementary school–aged children saw R-rated movies with her. On a whim, she got a tattoo. We're not sure if the kids went along for that field trip.

When school started, Darcy's vacation abruptly ended. Her

husband gave her an ultimatum. The spending had to stop or she had to go back to work. She chose to budget.

With Darcy on a budget and the children in school, she had to find other activities to occupy her time. She started volunteering at her children's school. Soon she was chairing every carnival and fund-raiser it hosted. She was working like she was trying to make partner.

The demands of her volunteer activities spilled over into her evenings and weekends. She had to hire a part-time babysitter because she was away so much. Within a few months, she was bitterly complaining.

"I had it easier when I was working, and I was paid for it," she groaned.

Once Darcy's initial euphoria over leaving the job she hated and her mini-vacation ended, she was dissatisfied with her life. She didn't like all the cleaning and cooking she had to do. She didn't see her children as much as she thought she would because they were occupied with school, sports, and dance classes. Plus she was busy with fund-raisers, which she didn't enjoy all that much because the other volunteers weren't as "professional" as she was.

"They don't take their duties seriously. Some don't even show up when they're supposed to," she complained. She questioned her place in the world. After months of swinging back and forth on the pendulum of depression and denial, she realized she needed a new profession. After a year of saving the money for tuition, she's now studying to become a psychologist.

We're not saying that you shouldn't enjoy yourself when you're at home with your child. For a lot of us staying home is more stressful than working outside the home. We need relaxation and down time. We should never feel guilty about taking that time or a spa day.

Be clear about why you're quitting. Don't simply make your

children an excuse for leaving an unpleasant work situation. If you realize you hate your job then make sure you know that's why you're leaving. Make a list of all your reasons for choosing to stay home. Be honest with yourself. Is there more to your decision than just wanting to take care of your children? If most of the items on your list relate to problems at work, consider the possibility that what you really need to do is find a new job. And, if you're still sure you want to quit and stay at home, knowing what is motivating you to leave your job now will help you figure out what job you would like when and if you decide to go back into the workforce later.

WHAT ARE YOUR EXPECTATIONS?

In addition to analyzing why you're really quitting, think carefully about what your expectations are when you do quit. Make sure that you aren't expecting too much from the experience, because if you do and you're disappointed, your family will suffer.

An analogy can be drawn to psychologists who interview patients undergoing organ transplants or gastric bypass surgery before clearing them for these procedures. The psychologist will ask a morbidly obese woman, for example, what she expects from a gastric bypass operation. If she says she expects it to completely change her life for the better, she isn't cleared for the operation, because while the surgery can improve her life, it isn't a panacea for all her problems. Instead, she's sent for counseling until the psychologist feels her expectations square with reality.

While your decision to stay home certainly doesn't fall in the same category as major surgery, the psychology is the same. If your expectations for the experience don't fit the reality of what's about to happen, you and your children will pay the price. For you, this may mean dealing with a period of disappointment and perhaps even depression later. For your children, it may result in them becoming anxious and acting out.

Carolyn is a woman who thrives on external motivators. She craves accolades from others, winning awards at work, and getting promotions. Before deciding to stay home with the kids, she had to take a long hard look at the reality of the situation.

"It dawned on me one day that I wouldn't have the same things that motivated me at work keeping me going at home," she said. "Clearly, my son wasn't ever going to heap praise on me for the exciting way I read him a bedtime story, and my daughter wasn't likely to present me with an award for driving her around town all week."

In the end, Carolyn decided to stay home, but she is careful to do it in a way that still meets her own needs for fulfillment. While her kids are in school, Carolyn participates in civic groups and community projects where she can still get a pat on the back every once in awhile and perhaps even win an award. By taking this approach, she is dealing with the reality of staying at home in a way that best fits her personality and is realistic as to her needs. Had she not taken this good hard look at herself in advance, she likely would have simply quit and been extremely disappointed with her life. Now Carolyn can plan her return to work at her own pace rather than desperately running back to work after a bad experience at home.

CUTTING THE CORD

Okay, so you've really thought about it and you definitely want to quit. The most important thing to know now is when is the best time to cut the cord.

When You're Pregnant for the First Time

Never act rashly during pregnancy because you don't know if it's the hormones talking or you. Spur of the moment is out. Slow down. Think it over for a week. At the end of the week, think it over for another week. If you still want to quit, don't. At least not right away. You have to devise a game plan.

Why would we say something so awful when you're absolutely sure leaving your job in two weeks is the absolute best thing for you and the baby? Because it's the hormones talking, unless you're in the absolute job from hell and you report directly to Satan or one of his agents on earth. But, if that's the case, why didn't you quit before? Yep, it's probably the hormones.

We say try to make it to the eighth month of pregnancy at least.

We say that for several reasons:

- You'll be bored out of your mind.
- You'll probably feel better with or need the extra money.
- You won't have any other mothers around you all day to talk to about the weird little stuff like your sense of smell going all wonky.
- It'll give you time to shore up things like the current information of important contacts for when you want to go back to work.
- You'll still have health, life, and disability insurance policies.

All those work hours can be useful for something other than work. Plus, you don't eat as much in the office as you do at home, so it's a built-in weight management program to boot.

Once you're resigned to showing up at work through swollen ankles and an itchy stomach, you have to figure out what you want to do after your pregnancy.

When You Already Have Children

It's a little easier to decide to quit after you've already had children. You know what it's like to balance work and family. You cried the first time you left your baby to show up at the morning meeting. You've done it.

When's the best time to leave? Never leave during the busy season. Give a month's notice. Do all the bending over backward necessary to make a good impression.

You have another advantage over pregnant women. You've proven you can work after you gave birth. People will know that when you want to go back to your job you'll be able to handle your family and career. That helps with the transition back to the working world.

When You Said, "I'll Be Back"

The stickiest situation of all is when you take maternity leave and you're absolutely or pretty darn sure you'll be back, but then you don't want to come back, or after a week back on the job you realize working isn't for you right now.

What do you do?

It depends.

If you're already back at work, tell your boss right away you don't think you'll be staying too long. Also tell her you'll stick it out for a couple months. Wait until the busy season is over. The holidays have passed. You've caught up on all the work that piled up while you were away and paid back a couple favors to colleagues who took on your load. Once a respectable period has elapsed—it could be a few weeks or a couple months—then tell your boss your time is up. Tell her you'll help find and train your replacement. Offer to work part time on projects if she needs help. Assure her that no matter how long it takes to find someone you'll stick it out. Do all this with a smile.

Leaving before you've paid your dues isn't pleasant. Take it from Dana.

Dana was absolutely positive that she'd bound back to work after giving birth. She was a financial analyst for a top investment firm and she loved what she did. She worked in a group of five people analyzing the retail sector. Each person in the group had a specialized area of expertise so there wasn't any overlap of duties. When Dana came back from eight weeks of maternity leave, the work was piled up because no one else in her team could do her job. As a result, many projects the team was responsible for were delayed until Dana caught up.

Dana had about sixty hours of overtime ahead of her in the next three weeks. On top of that she had fallen in love with her baby. She didn't want to go back to work, but she didn't want to disappoint her colleagues either. Her first week back she trudged into the office and hoped her conflicted feelings would evaporate. They didn't. To make matters worse, her colleagues, even the women on her team, were angry with her for being such a "girl." She needed to tough it out, they said.

She tried. In order to catch up on her backlog of work, she would nurse the baby at 3:00 A.M., go to work at 4:00 A.M., hot-foot it back home at 7:00 A.M. for another breastfeeding and shower, and hightail it back to the office by 9:00 A.M. This schedule allowed for about four hours of sporadic sleep a night. By the end of the week, Dana was dying. She pushed through the weekend, spending almost all her waking hours in the office. On Sunday night, when her breast pump stopped working and it didn't look like she had moved more than a couple inches of paper off of the mountain of files on her desk, she cracked. She decided that no job was this important. Monday she didn't go in. She slept late and turned off her cell phone. She quit. She's never talked to her former coworkers again, which closed off a large part of her networking pool. When she wants to go back to work, she knows she won't be able to call the people she worked with for the last three years of her professional life.

Granted, Dana's story is extreme, but it also could've been handled a little better. If she was a little more upfront with her bosses and got more help before her maternity leave, her meltdown might have been prevented. If she had gotten someone to fill in, she wouldn't have been so backlogged. If she had told her colleagues in person she wasn't returning, she might have salvaged a couple of relationships.

If you're not back at work yet and it isn't really an option to go back, be honest with your employer. Don't wait for your maternity leave to expire. Think of the position you're putting her in. She's most likely doling your work out to other employees and possibly doing some of it herself. When you quit, that will trigger a weeks- to months-long search for a replacement. She'll have to pore over résumés and spend a lot of time interviewing. It's best if you give her as much time as possible to prepare.

Talk to her in person. Tell her that you had every intention of coming back but as soon as that bundle of joy was put into your arms you knew you couldn't go back to work and put your child in someone else's arms. She'll understand or will in time, if you're upfront.

Offer whatever time you can to help train a replacement—

you know the usual groveling we recommend. Maybe she won't need your help at all, but she'll respect you for offering.

Sidney's baby was born prematurely and with several complications. She knew that the child would need all her time for several months. For at least a month, the baby would be in the hospital.

A week after she delivered she told the museum she worked for as a grant writer that she wasn't coming back. She explained the situation and told them she was sorry to give them such short notice. Her boss said to her, "Thank you for being so honest and considerate. We hope you will consider us in the future when you're looking for a job." That's the kind of exit you want.

Sometimes you don't have a choice. You have to go back for a year or more.

Monica had to go back.

Her maternity leave started in the twentieth week of her pregnancy when a routine sonogram revealed a problem that sent her straight to surgery and bed rest. She was out for six months.

Her law firm assured her they'd handle everything. Coworkers took over her incomplete files and open cases. At every turn in the road, her bosses worked hard to make sure she was taken care of. She owed her law firm big time.

She planned to go back shortly after giving birth. Unfortunately, Mother Nature wasn't on the same page. Monica gave birth ten weeks early. Her son spent the first seven weeks in the neonatal intensive care unit. When he was allowed to go home, he required daily medications for apnea and reflux. A daily dose of caffeine helped his breathing. He wore an apnea monitor, which only sounded once for a true emergency, but tended to go off frequently for false alarms. Monica kept extending her maternity leave.

Finally, her firm told her that if she wanted her slot she needed to come back.

Monica scrambled to find child care and hired a nanny. One day, over stifled yawns, the nanny let it slip that she was working two jobs. At night, the nanny stocked goods at a local sporting goods store. By day, she cared for Monica's premature infant with all of his special medications and apnea monitor.

"I sleep when he sleeps," she told Monica with a smile.

Translation: He is probably screaming his head off before Mom comes home while his nanny rests up for her night job.

With that piece of information, Monica did what any other responsible mother who abhors confrontation would do. She packed up the baby and left town until her husband could fire the nanny. The wisdom of that decision became clearer several weeks later when the local police department called looking for the nanny.

Still, Monica didn't quit. She kept working because she felt she owed a lot to the law firm. She worked there for two and a half years, until she knew her bosses and colleagues wouldn't resent her when she left.

We know that there are times when you feel you have no choice. You think you have to go back to work for a year or two when your heart is screaming to stay home with your baby. It's okay. Do what you have to do and then quit if you want. You have at least eighteen years with your child living under the same roof. You have plenty of time.

2
Feathering the Nest

How to Financially Prepare
Before You Quit

Quitting is about more than packing up your office and throwing away your pantyhose. Whether or not you're the main breadwinner, reducing your family income can have seismic impact. As soon as you think you may want to stay home with your child (even if it's a year before you get pregnant) you should make adjustments to your spending. You need to prepare yourself for the reality of the financial cost.

FEASIBILITY OF QUITTING

Those squirmy, adorable bundles of joy are expensive. Here are a few financial facts that will give you an idea of what you'll be spending.

- Parents spend $20,000 in the first two years of a child's life on average, according to the U.S. Department of Agriculture.
- Families making $70,000 or more will spend $353,000 on a child by his eighteenth birthday, according to the USDA.
- Consumer Credit Counseling Service suggests couples budget an increase of $200 a month with the arrival of a baby.
- A baby's health-care expenses in the first year of life are $4,000 on average, if he isn't covered by his parents' plan.
- On average women who take time off suffer a 17 percent loss in retirement savings and earning potential for every year they take off compared to their working peers.
- For a quick look on how child-care costs break down look at the "Raising a Child" calculator at www.baby-center.com.
- *Parents* magazine also has a quiz you can take, "Can You Afford to Quit Your Job?" To find out, go to www.parents.com/quiz/quitjob_0405.jsp.

Financial advisors recommend saving and getting your financial house in order a year before you have a child. Planning in advance could make the difference between being able to stay home with your baby and trudging reluctantly back to work.

WHAT TO DO FIRST

To figure out if you can stay home or not and for how long, you have to know your financial information better than you know

Britney Spears's love life. Once you determine where your money is going, you'll know if you can cut back your spending and by how much.

Sit down with all your monthly bills.

Sometimes it's better to do this with your husband, emphasis on the *sometimes*. If he's a big spender and needs to understand how much debt the two of you are in and what you need to do to save, then take him through it. Show him the large stack of papers and corresponding checks you're about to write. Scare him into saving.

Maybe he's the one who usually pays the bills and you need to figure out what's going on with the budget. You're the big spender. Buy yourself a bag of candy and force yourself to go step by step over the budget with him. Educate yourself. Think of this as the horrible prerequisite you have to take in order to graduate. Muscle through it. You'll gain some shopping willpower when you look at the credit card bill and truly understand how much of your money goes to shoes and manicures.

To get a handle on your expenses start with the basics. Get a notebook and at the start of the month write down every bill you pay. Make a list with columns for: the company you're paying the bill to; the monthly amount of the bill; the total balance remaining; and the interest rate charged.

Tally up all your bills in an *outgoing* column. Look at your bank statement and add up how much you take out each month at the ATM on average. Categorize what you're spending this money on, for example, entertainment, food, gas. Put the average ATM amount in your *outgoing* column as well.

Look at what your husband's and your net income is each month. Write those figures down in the notebook in an *incoming* column.

Subtract the *outgoing* column from the *incoming* column.

What do you have left? Be it two hundred or two thousand, you're going to use that money to start tackling debt and other financial necessities.

This is the hardest part. Getting the game plan together is like experiencing amateur dentistry without painkillers. You're confronting all the little and large mistakes you've made in the past few years—those beautiful boots you had to buy and never wear because they kill your feet. It's all in there and now you're taking responsibility for it. It doesn't feel good now but it will when you see a zero balance on the credit card.

If you need help figuring out your budget try the "How Much Am I Spending?" calculator at www.choosetosave.org.

CAN YOU QUIT?

It depends on how much debt you have, how many expenses you can cut down on, and what you're willing to sacrifice.

- Would you consider moving to a smaller and cheaper house farther away from town?
- What about trading in one of your cars for an older, less expensive model?
- How about cutting down on eating out?
- What about the somewhat financially risky move of using money gained from refinancing your mortgage to support your time at home?

Try living on just your husband's salary for at least two months. Put your paycheck in the bank and don't touch it. Is this doable? Were the sacrifices horrible? Or just a little unpleasant? Consider this: If your gross income is $30,000 a year or less, the family might be better off with you staying at home. Let's look at where your money is going. If you make $30,000 annually:

- $9,000 is taken out in income taxes
- $2,000 for work clothes and dry cleaning
- $3,000 eating out
- $3,000 in home repairs and housekeeping that you're not there to do because you're at the office
- $2,000 in parking fees, gas, and higher insurance costs because you're driving to work every day
- $1,000 for cell phones and computers
- $6,000 for each child for child care

That leaves you with $4,000. That means that $26,000 of a $30,000 salary is tied up in helping you work. So the question for you is: Can you cut $4,000 a year out of your budget? If you can't do that at the moment then make a plan so you can do it in a year or two years. Be patient. You'll feel better if you quit when your finances are in order.

You can begin by economizing. Create a budget you can comfortably live on. If you're ambitious and want to speed the process along, you could make some big sacrifices like moving to another city altogether. Life in Manhattan is quite a bit pricier than it is in Denver, Colorado. We know one woman who moved to Charleston, South Carolina, from Boston with her husband after the birth of their first child. They're both psychologists. They share a practice and work alternate days so they can take turns caring for their daughter. They hope to slowly ramp up her husband's hours and practice until they're comfortable that they can make it on his income alone. By moving they estimate they reduced what they need to live on in half, so instead of taking four years to achieve their goal they think it will take two.

There are several things you can cut down on while working that will speed up your ability to take time off, including car and house payments by opting to drive or move into something cheaper. You can also look at:

- Home and cell phone plans. Are there cheaper ones out there? Can you get away with fewer minutes? You could save a couple thousand dollars a year with some vigilance.
- Cable package. Can you do without HBO?
- Magazine or newspaper subscriptions. Do you read everything you get?
- Prepackaged food. It's a lot more expensive than making it from scratch.
- Heating and cooling. Try knocking your house's temperature down a degree in the winter and up a degree in the summer, you'll save. Or program your thermostat to automatically change when you sleep to save money.

The one thing we don't recommend is going part time as a way to save money. You won't. Most of the money you make will go into child care, probably at least $3,000 per child for part-time care. If you want to go part time as a way to keep your foot in the door, go ahead. It's a great way to keep up contacts. Just realize you probably won't be contributing much to the family income.

Since you're not quitting right away don't let everyone at work from your boss to the parking attendant know that you're even thinking of quitting someday because you might just change your mind. You want to keep your job if you do.

HOW TO SHORE UP YOUR FINANCES

The Game Plan

If you plan on working for a year or more before you quit, now is the time to start shoring up your debt. While you're working you should be aggressive in paying off debt with double-digit interest rates. Then focus on building up an emergency fund and maxing out your retirement.

Credit Cards

We all know that credit cards are killers. Most Americans carry an average of $8,000 in credit card debt. Before you quit your job make it your mission to pay off as much credit card debt as you can. The double-digit interest isn't doing you any favors and will bug you like cellulite in summer for the whole time you're not working. How many credit cards do you carry debt on? Give us the honest answer, not the one you admit to with your friends. We know it's ugly.

Debbie Marson, a financial advisor, recommends paying the minimum on the ones with the largest balances and paying as much as possible on the one with the smallest balance. Once you pay that one off shift your money to the card with the next highest balance.

"It's a psychological thing. You'll feel like you're accomplishing more if you reduce the number of credit cards you have debt on," she says.

It's true. There's nothing like writing that last check, tearing up the last bill on the credit card, and knowing that next month you won't be getting another one. It's simplifying your bill paying.

Another financial advisor recommended paying off the card with the highest interest rate first, then the next highest and so on.

Cancel credit cards as you pay them off. Ideally you should only have two credit cards you pay off each month. We say two because not all places take Visa or American Express so it's better to have both as long as you pay them off each month. Make sure you get credit cards with rewards that you convert to things like free plane tickets. J.C. traded her American Express points in for two first-class tickets to Paris. Some credit experts say that canceling credit cards doesn't help your credit rating, but that's not the point of canceling them. If you don't have them you're not tempted to use them.

Department store cards are basically worthless. They invariably have high interest rates and are brutal about tracking down payments. Get rid of these as quickly as you can.

Cutting down the number of cards you have and the interest on them helps your credit. Decreasing the cards you own also allows you to track your expenses more easily.

If you can't pay off your credit cards before you quit and you know it's going to be a few years before you're debt free, become an expert on zero-percent-interest offers. Switch your balances to the zero percent cards. Be vigilant. Track when the deals shift to high interest rates and switch cards. In the fine print of any credit card you sign up for it spells out how long you'll have zero percent interest on the card—usually between six months to a year. It also spells out that if you're late paying your monthly bill during that period you lose your zero percent. Some cards are sneaky and change the date your bill is due by a couple days from month to month to trip you up. It's easy to go online and look at when your bill is due and what interest rate your account is at. Most likely, you'll have to get new cards every four to six months. At least this way you'll only have to pay off your debt instead of heavy interest fees. Nothing hurts like looking at your credit card bill and realizing you're paying $200 in interest and $50 on the actual amount you owe. Highway robbery.

You can find lots of these offers in your mailbox. You probably receive a bunch of zero percent promises in the mail every week. File them away for later use. You can also look on the Internet for good credit card offers.

Emergency Fund

When you quit it's more important than ever to have at least three months of expenses—we know some experts say six months, but that may be unrealistic for a lot of us—socked away in a money market fund or a savings account because your husband's job will be the only income stream your family has. So if there's an emergency like a faulty transmission, nail in a car tire, or a dog eating poisonous Mountain Laurel pods, convulsing, and having to spend the night at the animal hospital (don't laugh, this happened to J.C.), you can dip into the three months fund rather than using the credit card. There are some credit cards like Care credit, which provide a $5,000 credit limit at zero percent interest for a year to use for veterinary and dental expenses.

Aubrey Ann Smith, a financial advisor, says money market funds or savings accounts are typically better than CDs because they allow you to withdraw money more frequently. If you want to take the CD route make sure you can pull out money at least once without being penalized.

You should also look into establishing a home equity line of credit. It's easily accessible, promises low interest rates, and is another solution if your emergency fund is tapped out. We also recommend pet insurance; veterinary hospitals can get expensive.

Your Retirement

Take advantage of your company's 401k while you can. Match your company's contribution but don't max out your retirement contribution unless you've paid off your credit card debt and built up an emergency fund.

If your company lets you keep your 401k with them and you're happy with the performance, keep the money where it is. If you're not, investigate funds to transfer your company retirement into once you quit. Think no-load mutual funds. Ask friends about their financial advisors. Talk to several professionals and find the person with whom you feel comfortable working. Expect to pay a fee to transfer.

Now is also the time to talk to your husband about his making contributions to a Roth IRA or another retirement vehicle for you while you're not working—well, not working for money.

Under current tax codes, the nonworking spouse can put a couple thousand a year into an IRA. Here's how it works now—although the rules do change. Assuming you and your husband file a joint return showing an adjusted gross income of $150,000 or less, you can make a deductible contribution of as much as $3,000 to your own IRA—or $3,500 if you're 50 or older. If your joint AGI is higher, multiply the amount over $150,000 by 30 percent (35 percent if you're at least age 50) and reduce the limit by that amount. Say your AGI is $154,000 and the nonworking spouse is 45. Then your deductible contribution would be limited to $1,800—that's $3,000 minus $1,200 (30 percent of $4,000). Not great, but at least it's something. If there's any way you can, you should do it. It's a tax-free way to save more money when your husband maxes out his retirement payments. Plus, it's not fair that all the retirement money is in his name.

Whatever contributions you can make to your retirement when you're not working are hugely important for several reasons (we know we're repeating ourselves but this is major). One of the biggest is compound interest. For example, assume that you generate an interest rate of 10 percent annually on your investments. That means roughly every seven and a half years you double your money. You want as many years to double your money as possible, so investing when you're younger is more important than trying to play catch up later.

Refinance Your Mortgage

Refinance your mortgage for the same number of years but get a lower interest rate, which means lower payments. This is helpful when the family income is decreased. Don't take money out to pay off debt, unless you really need to so you can stay home. Don't shorten the terms because you want to keep your payments as low as possible.

Cars

Some of you may be using a company car, so you'll have to buy a car when you quit. Think about how that will affect your budget. Ask yourself tough questions like, even though the car is a four-door sedan the size of a boat and looks like my grandmother should be driving it, is my company giving me good enough terms to buy it? Also, if you live near public transportation can you and your husband manage with one car?

We know it's a horrifying suggestion, but give it some thought. Obviously, if you live in a place like Texas or California or Nebraska where public transportation is an oxymoron this isn't an option for you.

Around large urban areas there are also programs like Zipcar, where you share a fleet of cars for a fee. You sign up for a membership, pay a thirty-dollar start-up fee, and are given a zip card. You make a reservation when you want to use a car, go to the designated spot where one of the cars is parked, usually in an apartment complex or college campus, hold your membership card up to the windshield to unlock it, and you're mobile. When you're done, you return the car to its designated parking spot. A car can be reserved with a few minutes' notice online. Fees range from $10 to $15 an hour and include gas, insurance, and XM satellite radio. You can check out www.zipcar.com for further information.

If none of these solutions works, start saving for a down payment. The bigger the down payment, the smaller the monthly payments. Negotiate while you still have a job. Look on eBay. A friend of ours won a great Audi station wagon for thousands less than its book value. It only cost $600 to ship it from Ohio to Oregon. It also had a great feature that you don't find in a lot of Oregon cars—seat heaters.

Life Insurance and All the Other Insurances

You most likely have life insurance through work, which you'll lose when you quit. Buy a new policy. If something happens to you, your husband is going to need lots of help to get through it, including time off and child care.

You'll also lose your disability insurance and, unfortunately, you don't qualify for it if you stay at home. Personally, that makes no sense to us because if you're hurt who's going to take care of the kids?

Make sure your husband has a good disability plan and that he's all paid up. Also, you may want to increase his life insurance. Financial experts recommend getting term insurance rather than whole life or universal life policies because term life is generally inexpensive compared to other types of policies. Many term policies promise to keep premiums at the same cost for twenty years. The stay-at-home parent should probably be insured for $250,000, which will cover child care and household debts. Premiums should be a couple hundred dollars a year. You should get life insurance that covers ten times the working parent's gross salary. That amount will give the stay-at-home parent about five years before he or she has to go back to work. Check out www.insure.com to research insurance rates.

We know lots of husbands who looked at their wives funny when they suggested this last bit. We know they were wondering if the request meant they'd be meeting with an untimely demise. If that's his reaction, remind him that the purpose of the policy is to make certain that if anything happens to him, his wife and children won't end up out on the street. Remind him, too, that you're conceding that a policy will need to be written for both of you, not just him. With that, any fear he might have about turning his back on you or urge he'll feel to sleep with one eye open should subside.

Ideally, before you get pregnant do research into your medical insurance as well as what your husband's company offers. Find out if your medical insurance covers prenatal care. Does it cover

sick- and well-baby visits? What delivery options are covered?
Research deductibles and co-pays. Find out how much it will cost
to add a dependent.

If you're thinking about switching plans, make sure the other
plan covers preexisting conditions if you're pregnant. To compare
health benefits of different medical insurers go to www.planfor
yourhealth.com.

Wills and Such

Everyone always says this whenever you do anything major in life
but it's true. Get the wills in order. This is especially important if
you or your spouse has children from another marriage and now
you're having children together. Get everything straightened out
on the front end. Designate who will take care of your children
in case you or your husband die.

Don't put the only copy of the will you have in a safe deposit
box. You can put the original in there. But make copies and let
your parents and best friends know where your important documents are in case anything happens. The reason for this—the
only person allowed to open your safe deposit box is the executor
of your will. If your will is in your safe deposit box there's no way
for someone to prove he or she is allowed to access it.

Allowances

This is a really touchy subject. We're warning you ahead of time.
You're a professional woman who is used to making her own
money. You've probably gotten a salary of your own since you
graduated college. It's an uncomfortable adjustment to have to

ask your husband for money. It's nearly impossible to explain to your husband why you spent fifty dollars on blush and lip gloss.

Discuss this subject in detail before you think about quitting. Get all the baggage laid out on the table. Things you'll be giving up: vacations with all the amenities; designer clothes; takeout food several times a week; regular massages; manicures and pedicures; lawn service; cable television premium channels. You get the idea.

When you give up some of these luxuries (e.g., lawn service and takeout), you or your husband will need to add more household duties to your repertoire. You should also learn the art of coupon clipping and comparison shopping. Granted it takes time and organizational skills, but you'll be pleasantly surprised by what you can save.

The biggest thing you have to agree on is that you don't have to ask for money. You shouldn't have to ask permission. The two of you are in this together, so you should have the same rights and rules.

That means if you have to ask permission to spend over $1,000 then so does he. Of course, things don't always work that way.

We noticed a putting green being rolled out in the backyard of our friend's house recently. The yard had been dug up and flattened. All rocks and stones had been removed and brand-new sod was being laid down. It looked incredibly expensive. We had no idea how much that would cost. Is that three pairs of Manolo Blahniks? A pair of diamond studs?

We casually mentioned to our friend, "Wow, that looks like a lot of work."

She replied, "Yeah, but it was such a deal, less than a thousand dollars."

A week later she called us up fuming. The construction of the putting green came in at seven thousand dollars. She only found out because she heard her husband talking to one of his friends.

Her husband hadn't told her the truth. We know we do it. We buy something we really want and fudge its cost so we don't cause marital strife. It only becomes a problem when the spending is generating a lot of debt that you can't pay off each month.

Keep in mind there will be a shift in the power relationship when who makes the money changes.

One woman we talked to started ironing her husband's shirts and doing his laundry when she stayed home. She also took a cooking course and catered to her husband's culinary tastes because she said she looked at staying home like a job. In her mind, assisting her husband with some of his needs was part of her responsibility.

Also, keep in mind that no husband in his right mind wants to stir up and continue to stoke conflict with the person who sleeps next to him at night. Men fear it. Most of the guys we know will lie, cheat, and steal to avoid full-on battles with their spouses. Expect one or two blowouts about major spontaneous purchases. But after a couple of arctic freeze-out nights, behavior modification will occur. He'll actually talk to you before he buys the car, iPod, fill-in-the-blank.

Strategies for Discussing Spending with Your Spouse

- If your husband's spending becomes a problem, try to identify the real issue. Is it that you're not working? He may feel that if you just went back to work this wouldn't be a problem. If that's the case, you'll need to go back to the original discussion about why you both agreed you shouldn't work in the first place.
- Don't begin by attacking him for spending too much. The natural human instinct in that circumstance is to

attack back or shut down and not hear you. Instead, approach him, remembering that you are teammates, not opponents.

- Gather all your data. Be prepared to show him the family expenses for the past few months and the family's resulting financial picture.
- Take a team approach in talking to him. Say "I'm worried about our expenses." Use words like *we*, *our*, and *us* in your conversation.
- Remind him of your individual roles on the team. Use a football analogy. You're an offensive lineman, and he's the quarterback. Each needs the other for the team to win.
- Listen to his concerns and offer constructive suggestions in response. Be willing to offer compromises, but don't bring up things you would never really consider like switching roles or working part time.

Don't worry if you fight more than usual at first. Remember your first year of marriage. You were adjusting and readjusting the power dynamic, how to keep your individuality while being a couple and who does what around the house. This is a lot like that; it's a time to redefine the relationship and make claims on power. Know that this too shall grind itself into a reasonably healthy version of a relationship.

HOW TO CUT DOWN

We know it's hard to do when you have to buy baby stuff and maternity clothes, but there are areas you naturally will be cutting down on and other areas where you can cut down spending with some effort. For example, you won't be drinking when you're pregnant so that's a cost saver unless you decide to throw yourself a 'Ritas and Rattles baby shower like a friend of J.C.'s did. Never heard of one? They're all the rage in Texas. The 'ritas are margaritas, which are served at a cocktail party kind of co-ed shower. Needless to say, there's drinking at the showers, and they're expensive to throw.

You can also cut down on how much you go out to eat. For the first trimester you'll be throwing up a lot anyway so you might as well eat cheaply. You can cut down your cable package. Doctors usually advise pregnant women not to drink a lot of coffee or any other caffeinated beverage so you won't be going to Starbucks every morning. You'll be saving three or four bucks a pop.

Baby Gear

Baby stores are filled with gadgets like head cradles to make it easier for your baby to sleep in the car seat. By the way, nine times out of ten the head cradles are completely useless and hard to maneuver into the car seat. Most babies, like adults, will droop their heads forward, not to the side, where the head cradle is, when they sleep. The point? There are a lot of useless things out there that you can save money on by not buying.

Sleep Positioners

Designed to help keep the baby resting on his side and thus in theory reduce the risk of SIDS (clearly a worthwhile goal), these products rarely work as intended. Monica tried a few of these and frequently checked on her son during a nap only to find him sleeping peacefully on one end of the crib and the sleep positioner on the other.

Bassinet

You don't need it. Unless your baby is Tom Thumb, he will fit in it for about three months and then you're stuck with a $100 albatross.

Toys That Clip onto the Car Seat or Stroller

We've never seen a baby play with those brightly colored intellectually stimulating toys. We see adults jiggle them around. We've even seen dogs go for them. But no babies, not a single one, has ever been captivated by them for more than five seconds. Babies seem to be a lot more interested in crinkly paper.

Monogrammed Bibs and Burp Cloths

No doubt you will need plenty of bibs and burp cloths. What you don't need is to get carried away buying them. One good meal, particularly the strained peas and carrots or mystery meat entree, and you'll wish you'd saved your money and bought something cheaper.

Hooded Towels

Your baby will look like the Gerber baby all wrapped up in his beautiful hooded fifty dollar bath towel with the zebra stripes and

ears attached to the hood. Problem is the hooded towels are usually much thicker than other baby towels and thus bulkier and
harder to handle when carrying a squirming child from his bath
to the changing table. Also, with any luck, your baby will continue to grow. After just a few short months, the baby's hooded
towel will be useless unless he's headed to the Sahara Desert and
needs something to keep his head and neck covered.

Clothes

We know they're incredibly cute and it's hard to resist buying
pink ballerina outfits, but please refrain. Go to used clothing
stores or garage sales. See if any friends with babies older than
yours would like to part with their used clothes. We bet they will.
And it's not like your child will know the difference between first-
and third-generation sleepers. Only get a few outfits in each size
because your baby will grow out of them quickly. Rely on the
grandparent factor. We'll talk more about it a little later.

Fancy Stroller or Car Seat

If you have the money and like the status (we like designer
brands just like everyone else) go for it. If you don't, the generic,
government-approved one is just as good. The biggest things the
fancy ones have going for them is they've been featured in *US
Weekly* with a celebrity mom. You are most likely not a celebrity
trying to keep up with your peers. Plus, those big pricey strollers
aren't lightweight or easy to assemble. They're bulky, heavy, and
could sever a toe if you're not careful. That means they're not for

those of us who have maybe one free hand to get the stroller from compact to road worthy before our babies start crying.

Soothing Chairs

From the moment a newborn belts out his first inconsolable wail we mothers become obsessed with finding ways to calm him. For some reason rocking and vibrating are the Ambien of the infant set. Soothing chairs promise to vibrate your baby into sweet sleep oblivion. Unfortunately, they don't always work. Monica knows this firsthand. She bought every model on the market. Her baby still screamed his head off, only now he was strapped down in a vibrating chair. He looked like the victim of shock therapy. Her mother told her to put the baby on top of the dryer because its vibrations should calm him. Didn't work. He kept crying, only now he was on top of a dryer in a less than attractive little room. Monica found that the car was the surefire sleep inducer. As soon as she put him in and drove a couple miles he was sound asleep. Granted, it can be tricky to remove a sleeping infant from a car but if you're motivated and sleep deprived enough you can contort yourself into any position needed. A car is a very expensive baby accessory, but we assume you have one anyway.

Shoes

Babies don't walk. Babies like to put their feet in their mouths. They don't like things on their feet. Do you know how many baby socks we've found littering the ground because junior didn't want them on? Plus babies don't really have ankles to help keep socks

up. Given all this information, shoes and fancy socks are a big
waste of money. We know they're cute. They're miniature, wee little things. Tiny Timberland boots, patent-leather Mary Janes, and
frilly lacy socks are precious and expensive, not practical.

Baby Wipe Warmers

Read any new mother guide these days or baby shower wish list
and you'll see baby wipe warmers make the Top Ten list. In spirit,
they remind us of the warm washcloths they put on your face at
the spa. Getting baby accustomed to spa treatments is fine.
What's not so great is paying for the privilege. Sure, it's only
twenty bucks, but twenty bucks here and there adds up. It's a
nonessential item. Do yourself a favor and quiz your friends on
what other things they find not worthy of owning. Some of our
friends swear that bottle warmers are totally useless. Others say
that the bouncy swings weren't worth the bother. Several say the
baby bathtubs are a waste of time. They prefer the inflatable
bather that fits into the bathtub. Other controversial items include: remote baby fever monitors, crib CD players, expensive
cribs, and silver rattles. We recommend evaluating all of these
items and after a thorough vetting deciding on a couple to try.
You can always buy more later if you find you need them.

Maternity Clothes

Go to used clothing stores. Look on eBay. Check out consignment shops and Goodwills in the nice part of town. Ask girlfriends if they still have their clothes. You'll find you will wear the

HOW TO VET BABY GEAR

- Ask your mother and siblings and friends with kids what they liked.
- Check out books like *Baby Bargains* by Denise Fields and Alan Fields and *The Girlfriend's Guide to Baby Gear* by Vicki Iovine and Peg Rosen. Monica loved both of these.
- Peruse *Consumer Reports Best Baby Products*. It's a great resource for newborn baby gear.
- Pick the items that multiple people list as their favorites.
- On items that get mixed reviews, it's a judgment call. Do you really want it? If it doesn't break the bank get it.

same favorite pieces over and over again. Pregnancy clothing lasts for fewer days than the most time-sensitive fads. We know one woman, Jessica, who learned the hard way. She decided she wasn't going to be one of those women who wear stretched-out cotton shirts and ill-fitting sweatpants. She invested in $200 sequined strapless tops and low-rider designer jeans. She shelled out $500 for fluttery cocktail dresses. Jessica diagrammed out glamorous pregnancy outfits for nine months. Know what happened? Midway through her pregnancy she reverted to the cotton shirts and sweatpants because they were comfortable and she wasn't a movie star who had to worry about photo shoots. No matter how much of a fashionista you were in your previous life, pregnancy turns you into a creature who craves comfort.

Economizing Purgatory

If it's torture for you to economize like this, allow yourself one big splurge. Look at it at night. Fawn over it. Promise yourself you won't do it again. Monica's splurge was a Kate Spade designer diaper bag. She loved it. She ogled it adoringly when there was no designer item she could fit into. It gave her solace when she went out to lunch and saw sleek, slender never-been-pregnant women with flat stomachs and skinny thighs prance by. She took comfort in owning and carrying one pretty thing—other than the baby—with her at all times. Choose your splurge wisely. Make sure you get maximum usage from your object of desire.

The Grandparent Factor

We can't emphasize enough how much your parents and in-laws will fawn over you and the grandchild to be, especially if it's the first grandchild. Assuming you're on good terms with your parents, it's almost like they've had a direct infusion of pregnancy hormones. They become emotional and irrational.

One grandmother we know got so into her granddaughter that she hired her decorator to design the little girl's room. We're talking built-in bookshelves, coordinating bed linens, and rose-themed accents. It was nicer than the rest of the house.

Another grandmother purchased a tiny white fur coat with pom-poms for her new granddaughter. The baby and her parents lived in Florida but came up to New York for Christmas.

Trust us, any kind of cute and totally impractical object will be like catnip for grandparents.

They may have more time to check out garage sales and sales

at stores. More importantly, there's a little known fact about grandparents: They have a hidden network. Their friends bought toys, car seats, and high chairs for their grandchildren for their visits. The stories of these visits are what prompted your parents to ask you again and again when you were going to have children. Now it's payback time.

Your parents' friends' grandchildren have outgrown the stuff and they're looking for a place to dump it. You could be that place. You deserve it for all the unnecessary attempts to jump-start your biological clock. You know what we're talking about—the annoying phone conversations that invariably wound their way around to the subject of your fertility and understanding of sex, especially of how babies are made.

Other Ways to Save

Take your lunch to work. If you spend just six dollars a day on going out to lunch for thirty years you waste $100,000. If you have an expense account, that's a different story, by all means live it up while you can.

If you're a card writer, choose personal note cards instead of birthday cards. Note cards are about $1 each. Birthday cards cost up to $5 each.

Look for sales. Some Web sites let you know what stores have the best deals on certain items each week. Web sites like www.cairo.com track advertised sales at stores like Target and Wal-Mart. You can also get information on sales items at www .Froogle.com.

Sign up for an automobile safety class. Doing them can reduce your car insurance premium by at least 5 percent. Yes, they're boring, but you can take them by renting DVDs. Plus, when you do it you'll feel dorky and responsible, almost parental—in a good way.

When you do go out to eat, take advantage of the cards offered, where if you buy ten you get one free. Lots of sandwich shops offer these deals. You might not be a sandwich person now, but when you're pregnant you migrate toward comfort foods. Every day during Monica's second pregnancy, she'd stop by a café and grab a piece of cake. She saved a lot by getting every tenth slice free.

None of this sounds sexy. When we see people get their sandwich cards punched at the deli we judge. How can any normal human remember to bring their card to the deli? How do they keep hold of it? We think they must be anal-retentive accountant stereotypes because we can't keep track of such things, at least not in our typical day-to-day life. But this isn't normal life. This is life in savings mode. All bets and jokes are off.

3
Departure Strategies

Leaving the Office Door Open and Smoothing Over Family Relations

When you announce you're quitting your job, it'll feel like an emotional bomb went off in your life. You'll feel ripples in every relationship. Coworkers, family members, and friends will all have their own bedrock beliefs about what you should do. Some will subtly lobby you to try to win you over to their views. Others will all-out assault you. They might even call you stupid. A segment of your support network will support you wholeheartedly.

There are two tricks to navigating the next few months—figuring out who owns what opinion and how to leave each person and situation positively, meaning no blood loss or screaming matches. Avoiding unpleasantness, even if you have to hold your tongue in some instances, is important for a couple reasons. You can't fire your family. You need your friends. The coworkers will help you when you want to go back to work.

In a sense you need to craft a public relations strategy. You have to figure out what motivates all the different people in your life and then decide how to interact with them.

WHEN'S THE BEST TIME TO BREAK IT TO THE BOSS?

Bosses are people we all have to "handle." From day one at the job we try to ferret out common interests, passions that can be turned into Christmas presents, for example, a love of chocolate, and other ways to win their affections so that when a job opens up we will be promoted.

Bosses can be touchy about pregnancy.

A lot of them view it as a wrecking ball that crashes through their calm division of labor and schedules. Many of them are going to think that as soon as you announce you're pregnant, you're mentally checking out. They think you'll be a bundle of hormones and sickness. That you're just as likely to surf the Internet for cribs as do real work. They think this is another problem in a long litany of problems that they have to deal with throughout the day, except this is a nine-month ticking time bomb of a problem. You are an inconvenience to them.

Others will be more encouraging. They'll give you everything you ask for and more. When you have a boss like that do everything you can to continue to work for her, and if you quit, stay in contact. Those bosses are hard to find. They're keepers.

One male architect we talked to said his firm has the attitude that if you get pregnant and leave the firm you are somehow deserting the firm, but if you cut down on work because you are sick or a parent is dying it's okay.

A vice president at a toy manufacturer said that pregnant women think they are the only ones who have ever been with child before. They act like there should be a bubble of sensitivity around them at all times. They take advantage of their situation. They give in to morning sickness and constant tiredness too easily, pawning their work off on others.

"You won't tolerate the kind of absenteeism you get from pregnant women from anyone else," she said.

Whenever a woman comes into her office and breaks the news that she's going to have a baby, the boss inwardly cringes because she knows that she's going to have to shift time-sensitive work to other employees. If the woman has some form of morning sickness, which she probably will, she won't be in the office on a regular basis. She starts racking her brain on what's the better option—to hire a temporary employee or try to do without while the employee is on maternity leave. Then there's the issue of waiting while the woman is on maternity leave to see whether she'll come back to work or not.

"It's a major headache," she said, "The world doesn't stop because you conceived."

So, when is the best time to announce the news to your boss? Once you've planned it all out.

By planning, we mean decide, as much as you can, what you want: Are you not going back to work? Do you want to try part time? Do you want to work on special projects occasionally? Do you want to work with the company again in the future?

If you said yes to any of these questions figure out how to pitch these scenarios to show how they will benefit your boss.

For example, Lisa, an environmental consultant for an engineering firm, figured out that her firm needed her connections with the Environmental Protection Agency. She knew that they needed her to travel. She realized that they had a lot invested in her career because they had made her partner a year before she got pregnant. She came up with a plan that allowed her to take six months off, go back to work part time, and travel when required. She scheduled a meeting with her boss, presented her requests in writing, and reminded him of her relationship with the EPA. She told him she felt strongly about committing time to her child before he went to nursery school and would return to work full time in three years. The boss went for it because Lisa is an incredibly hard worker and the firm had done part time for another woman a year before and it went very well.

When she got pregnant with her second child, Elaine, a human resources specialist, decided to leave work. The children were going to be only fifteen months apart. She thought with two little ones at home, working full time would be insane. Plus she wanted to be part of their personality-forming years. She broke the news to her boss over lunch when she was four months pregnant. She told her she'd help find a replacement and work for as long as the company needed. She only asked for one thing— quarterly dinners with her boss to keep up to speed on the industry. Elaine knew she'd want to come back someday.

Diane, an accountant, knew as soon as she found out she was pregnant that she wanted to stay home with her child. She had her babies' names picked out when she was in junior high and she stuck with them—Madeline and Sam. She told her boss she was pregnant at three months and that she wouldn't be coming back after she gave birth. She offered to work during tax season as an independent contractor and when they needed extra help in general. She offered to accept a pay rate that was cheaper than her hourly salary and pointed out it was an even better deal than at first glance because it wouldn't include benefits.

All these women had a few traits in common:

- They knew their company's policies on pregnancies and maternity leave.

- They wrote up their own proposals.
- They framed their ideas in relation to what was in the best interest of their bosses.
- They didn't promise more than they could deliver.
- They asked for structured time to talk to their bosses.
- Their bosses were the first at work to know about their pregnancies.

Never tell your coworkers before your boss. You don't want to take the chance that someone might accidentally let your boss know before you tell her or that your boss will find out you told the whole office before you told him. No one likes to be the last one to be let in on a secret. Think PR. It's all about how the news is presented.

Callie brought cupcakes with little babies on them to work to announce her pregnancy. Danica sent out an animated e-mail with a crawling baby. Fiona invited colleagues to lunch.

You need to reassure your boss that you'll be a hundred percent while at work. You have to tell her you'll help find your replacement. You'll work for however long he needs you to. You'll juggle while you pour coffee and tap dance.

Don't let your boss know you're nauseous and tired if you can help it. Trust us, we've talked to lots of bosses who tell us as soon as they hear a woman's pregnant they write her off. They shift assignments to other coworkers. Prove them wrong. If you do, it will help your friends and later on your daughters. You're helping define how people view pregnant working women. Make all of us look good.

Don't use pregnancy as a perennial sick day. We interviewed one woman, Ally, who was incredibly nauseous during her second pregnancy. She tried saltines, ginger ale, acupuncture, and even medication, but nothing worked. She threw up all the time. She had to go to the hospital twice to get rehydrated. All this drama was swirling around her health but no one at work knew it. She showed up on time and participated in all meetings. She accomplished projects ahead of schedule. Ally said the biggest differences people around her noticed were that she went to the bathroom a lot (to throw up) and her breathing was deeper. She says that changing her breathing did the most to alleviate the nausea.

As soon as she gave birth the nausea went away. Ally says dealing with an infant seemed like a breeze after living with perpetual sickness.

We're not saying you have to go to the lengths Ally did, but you need to be a little stronger than normal.

If you're sure you're not coming back, don't take maternity leave.

Sure it might be tempting to get that extra money but your colleagues will resent you and your boss won't be too happy either. Really and truly this is the number one pet peeve of bosses and companies everywhere. Women say they're coming back and then they don't. They sap money and productivity from the company in two ways. One, there's the money the company pays in salary and health insurance during the leave. Two, there's the money and time it's costing the company to keep the slot open for the woman to return to work. Who do you think does the work when you go away? That's right, your ever-cheery colleagues. They are the very people you may want to network with when you go back into the workforce. If you leave them in the lurch, they won't be so happy to help. So as soon as you know you're not coming back let your boss know.

That said, if you don't know if you're coming back and your boss is hassling you about it, be honest. Tell him you're torn and you're trying to make the best decision possible. Assure him that as soon as you know what you want to do, he'll know.

"WHY ARE YOU THROWING UP IN MY TRASH CAN?"

Morning sickness and mood swings are big hints to coworkers that you're pregnant. As soon as our friend Jill took a bite of toast in the morning she knew she had twenty minutes before she threw up. She raced to her car and sped to work. Ironically, she worked at a food manufacturer.

She learned what time the parking lot was most isolated—8:25 A.M. She figured out exactly where to park so that she would have access to enough trashcans to throw up in between her car door and the front door to the building. She discovered the location of empty offices in case she couldn't quite make it to her desk in time.

Once she safely reached her office, she would close the door, sit at her desk, take deep breaths, and remain planted there until the waves of nausea passed. She initiated a policy that excluded her from morning meetings, which is a big hint to the pregnancy informed. She told her secretary she worked best on her computer in the mornings even though that hadn't been the case a month ago.

On one occasion her secretary found her taking a nap at her desk. Her head was tilted back and a full-throated snore emanated from her mouth.

The secretary shook her awake.

"You're pregnant, aren't you?" she asked excitedly.

She swore her secretary to secrecy.

It was tough going. A few times a day the secretary popped into Jill's office to talk about the pregnancy. Jill's concentration suffered as her desire to talk about the merits of breast- versus bottle-feeding rose.

She noticed the secretary gossiping with other employees and looking her way a couple times. She knew it was a matter of days before the whole office knew, so she spilled the news. Turns out most of the office already figured it out and it wasn't because of the secretary. Seems her vomiting wasn't as discreet as she thought it was.

Rather than being found out, like Jill, it's best to do a preemptive strike. Tell people you're pregnant before you start to show or throw up in the company trash bins. This way you can control the spin.

COWORKER PSYCHOLOGY

Your coworkers are hugely important in your returning to work someday strategy.

When you've been out of work for a couple years an e-mail to old coworkers can bring you up to date on what's going on in your industry. At a casual lunch, they can peruse your résumé and edit out old-fashioned language. Even if you think you'll never go back into the same industry, it's good to have options, so don't upset them when you exit.

You'll probably know you're going to leave for a few months before you actually do. During the remaining weeks you have left in your job you can reposition yourself. Write down a list of the people you work with: Next to each name jot down the relationship you'd like to have with that person before you quit. Next to that write a couple of specific things you can do to achieve that relationship (e.g., have coffee together once a week). Look at the list throughout the week to keep your goals present when you're at work.

Candace did this and turned around a rocky relationship with a coworker who had held a grudge against her for years. The coworker hadn't liked Candace since she overheard Candace gossip about what she was wearing at an office party. Ever since then, the woman went out of her way not to do Candace any favors, including not giving her the notes or even an oral summary of a meeting Candace missed.

"We had a cold war brewing for years," Candace said.

That all changed over a period of weeks. Candace began by complimenting what the woman was wearing. At first, the woman looked at Candace suspiciously, remembering Candace's previous criticism of her clothes, but Candace kept it up. Eventually the woman looked pleased by the compliments. Candace took things a step further and invited the woman to lunch and they found they had a few things in common. They loved yoga and harbored a mutual disdain for their current boss. They formed a friendship that was crucial to Candace when she returned to work a few years after quitting to stay home with her children.

In addition to forging closer relationships with your coworkers, you should assure each one of them you're not going to slack off. If you take maternity leave you should square as much away before you go as possible so they don't have much to cover you on. Now is the time to start storing up favors and the goodwill of the whole office: Do the undesirable assignments; come in early and leave late; restock the printer paper or make the community coffee; bring in doughnuts for everyone in the morning.

People remember your exit. You want to leave them with a good impression because when you want to go back to work these are the people you'll probably be calling.

COWORKER RIVALRY

Coworkers are best compared to siblings. You didn't choose them but you have to live with them. You may have been blessed with some you truly love and would voluntarily hang out with in your off hours, or you may be cursed with the kind where you wish you could limit your interactions to once-a-year visitations. Many will fall somewhere in between the two ends of the spectrum.

We're warning you that there are pregnancy-specific coworker traits that only become readily apparent after you announce your news. Pregnancy brings out all kinds of complicated emotions in just about everyone, though they won't admit it. To some it makes you the walking wounded, vulnerable to professional attack. To others you become more relatable and sympathetic.

There are a few tried-and-true classifications that we and many of the women we interviewed encountered. We list them below.

Breeds of Coworker

The Hungry Wolves

These are the young and childless. Their mindset is that the longer you work, the harder and better you're working. They pride themselves in staying at the office until seven or eight or later and then going out as a group for drinks until late in the evening. They like to regroup over the weekend and go to baseball games or get together on Sunday nights for dinner and to talk office politics. They eat, breathe, and sleep work.

Amanda was part of this cohort until she got pregnant. Then

her work style seemed like an endurance contest she no longer wanted to compete in. It was way too focused on career. When she started to pull back, her coworkers saw her as a liability—someone who was no longer a player. The more cutthroat of the group sniffed opportunity and used her condition as a wedge to pry her away from her job. They talked up her "lack of commitment" and made the boss believe she was no longer invested in her job.

The best way to deal with these people is to directly confront aggressive behavior. You should lay groundwork with your boss so when the person approaches him he has some ammo to combat their complaints. Let the passive-aggressive stuff they do roll off of you. You wouldn't think of waving your hand in an alligator pit to see if it's feeding time; think of that next time you want to trade barbs at the cubicle wall with a slimy colleague.

Den Mothers

These are the other young mothers, the women who have had children in the last five years and are still intimately familiar with the shift you are going through. They balance child care and work with varying degrees of success, depending on the day, just like the rest of us. They have developed an informal support group where they pick up the slack for one another, often without even being asked. They see the look of harried desperation in one another's eyes and know. They nod their heads and fill in.

Before you were pregnant you probably looked at these women with a touch of pity and incomprehension. Pity because they always looked so stressed and unkempt. Incomprehension because you had no idea why and what they talked so avidly to each other about. Now you know. Hopefully these women will take you out to lunch and kvetch about the trials of working while lugging around thirty extra pounds, how children handle it when you work, and how they dealt with their husbands during pregnancy and after.

Grizzly Bears

These are the women who didn't have children and have always resented the pregnant women prattling on about lower back pain and mothers running out early to catch a soccer game. They roll their eyes when they hear you're pregnant because you've now joined the cult of motherhood. They think you're no longer reliable or interesting to talk to (because they assume all you'll talk about is baby names).

It's best to keep a completely professional face with these women. Venture into discussing your personal life at your own risk.

Old Codgers

There are still men out there who remember the good old days as the time when women were only allowed to be secretaries and school teachers. In their minds, your pregnancy is another reason women shouldn't be allowed to be corporate leaders or professionals. They may even say something to that effect to your face.

The best response to this mindset is smile and walk away. You're not going to change these guys' minds so save your breath and don't debate them. Don't try to educate them. You'll walk away frustrated and tired. Save your energy for something worthwhile like walking to the coffee shop (though you won't be getting coffee as often now that you're pregnant) with another colleague. You can vent and get something good to eat.

Before They Take a Bite

Of course not all women or men will neatly fall into these categories, so how do you tell which is which? Wolf from coconspirator?

There are a few basic giveaways:

- Do they have children? It doesn't matter if you're the closest friends before you were pregnant. A woman who has never been with child won't understand constant nausea and a perpetual desire to take a nap.
- Is she sixty or older? This isn't always true, but it seems like some women who struggled for equality in the workplace (more than today's crop of twentysomethings and thirtysomethings) resent the way younger women may handle work and family. They don't like how we seem to glide into jobs or how we don't tough it out at work when we have children like they did. Not the most understanding person to share a cubicle with.
- Did you compete for a job? Unless she is your best friend there are probably still some feelings that she should've gotten your job—and she may still want it.
- Is he competitive about everything? If he takes lunchtime basketball like it's the Cuban Missile Crisis, beware. He may look at your job like the next battle he has to wage.

Now that you have an idea of what you're in for you can plan how to tackle the new landscape of office politics. There's only one more thing you really need to prepare for—what goes on when you're not at the office.

WHAT HAPPENS WHEN YOU'RE AT THE DOCTOR'S OFFICE

You think you're sailing along with your pregnancy. You've had some morning sickness, been a little groggy at morning meetings, and nodded off a couple times at your desk. No big deal. You've kept up with your work. You've been pleasant with everyone even when your hormones were telling you to rip off your cubicle neighbor's head because he brought smelly fast food to his desk two days in a row. You've managed to return everyone's e-mails even when you couldn't remember what you were supposed to pick up at the grocery store on the way home from work.

You think to yourself, Not too bad. I could breeze through this pregnancy thing.

Then you call in sick one day or you go to a doctor's appointment. That's when it hits. Passive-aggressive coworker revenge. Anything you've let slide in the past few weeks, anything that can be exaggerated to the coworker's benefit will be brought to the boss's attention the second you're gone.

He'll slink into the boss's office with that "I really like Suzie and I hate to say this but . . ." attitude and then he'll launch into the litany of things you've done wrong. He'll build a convincing case as to why you're incompetent. He'll ask that some responsibility be taken away from you for your own good and for the good of the office. He'll sound understanding and offer to help in any way possible, meaning he'll take over your choice assignments. Sure he'll have to work later, but he doesn't mind. It's for the good of the team, meaning in a few months he'll use his added responsibilities to angle for a raise or a promotion or your job.

Your boss will be troubled. Pregnancy is the Switzerland of job performance—he has to be neutral about everything you do until after you deliver the baby. He'll debate whether or not and how to say anything to you. You are in a fragile state and he's in a delicate position. If you're friendly with your boss, he may take you to lunch and have a heart to heart there. If you're not, he may not say anything to you but work behind the scenes to change your duties. When he starts to say things to you like "No, no don't worry about that. Roger will take care of that. You already have enough on your mind," you're in real trouble. A passive-aggressive coworker injected poison into your career, and it's starting to take hold.

PUTTING YOUR PUBLIC RELATIONS MACHINE IN HIGH GEAR

It's preferable to nip passive aggression in the bud, take charge, and talk to your boss before your colleague gets the chance. If you're out a lot because of morning sickness, tell your boss you're sorry about your absences. Explain what measures you've taken to make sure you're getting the work done. Do it early on so your boss has a ready-made answer to the backbiting colleague when he walks into the boss's office and closes the door.

If you've been outmaneuvered, do damage control. Take your boss aside and tell him that you know you've been a little out of it lately, but you're fine now and if you're ready to take on motherhood, you can handle any assignment he throws your way.

Show him in actions too. If you've slacked a bit, get back on the ball.

Head gossip and unflattering rumors off at the pass or at least quash them before they have a chance to take hold. Confront the passive-aggressive coworker. Tell him you've been a little sick but you're feeling much better now so thanks for the sympathy and offers of "help" but you don't need any. Stay late a few nights and make sure people see you.

Leah was given a promotion instead of a female coworker shortly before she became pregnant. When Leah was in her second trimester she found out her old coworker, now her employee, spread rumors that Leah was incompetent, didn't have the needed expertise, and was sleeping on the job. The woman had cataloged every time Leah had been late to work in the past couple of months and sent out e-mails to other employees with the subject line, "Leah Watch—Does she ever work?"

When Leah found out what rumors were swirling around her she called the employee into her office. Leah told her, "I hear you don't think I'm qualified for this job and you don't like me. I have this job. You report to me. Either find someone you like to work for, or stay here and shut up." The woman did keep quiet for the next week and then she quit.

"That was the best thing I could've done. It sent a message to everyone else that I wouldn't tolerate a rumor campaign," she said.

HOW TO PREPARE YOUR FAMILY

This can be almost as tricky as dealing with your coworkers.

Your husband and you should have discussed all the angles about your staying home months before you quit. There are huge financial, emotional, and power implications that need to be

A SHORT LIST OF WOMEN'S RIGHTS UNDER THE
1978 PREGNANCY DISCRIMINATION ACT

- An employer cannot fire, demote, or refuse to hire a woman because she is pregnant or may become pregnant;
- Pregnancy must be treated like any other employee disability or medical condition;
- Women on maternity leave cannot be denied benefits— accrued vacation time, seniority, raises, etc.;
- Under the federal Family and Medical Leave Act, mothers (and fathers) are entitled to twelve weeks of unpaid leave. More information is available at the EEOC's Web site (www.eeoc.gov) or by calling 800-669-4000.

hashed out far ahead of time, including the drop in family income, whether you get an "allowance," and the division of household chores. We'll discuss these in detail in later chapters.

Your own mother may be a factor. She is deeply invested in one of two scenarios. Either she wants you to be home for your kids, like she was or wanted to be. Or she wants you to work, like she did or wished she had. You have to prepare her for what you decide to do. Tell her after you've charted out all the details with your husband so you can provide her with specific answers to all the questions she'll raise. Let her know how important this decision is to you and how important it is to have her full support. Then tell her you have to go if you sense she's not supportive. Give her a day or two to absorb your decision and then talk to her again. If she's still not supportive, be patient. How long did it take her to warm to your husband? That could be the kind of timeline you'll have to deal with in gaining her acceptance of your decision.

When Diane, a primary care doctor, decided to stay home with her children, her mother practically set up an intervention. Diane's mother, a physician, worked and was proud to have laid the groundwork for her daughter and other women. But she wasn't ready to accept the possibility her daughter might not want to take up the gauntlet. She raged.

Christmas that year was so tense that Diane made sure to sit at the opposite end of the table from her mother during dinner. Her mother stooped so low as to give Diane an oven mitt as a gift since she'd have plenty of time for baking now. Things have cooled off some, but the subject of Diane staying home is by no means a safe one.

Diane skirts the issue when possible. She assures her mother she'll go back to work in a couple of years. She keeps all her licenses current. It's not ideal, but it's functional.

Gretchen's mother-in-law has proven to be a problem for her. The mother-in-law worked throughout her children's youth and she can't understand what a perfectly smart woman would do at home. She also thinks it's too much of a strain on her son to be the only breadwinner in the family. She's constantly cornering Gretchen and asking her when she's going to go back to work. The husband isn't much help. He hasn't ever stood up to his mother. Gretchen employs a lot of defensive maneuvers like changing the subject, going to bed early, and avoiding visiting her.

PREPARING YOUR FRIENDS

In this situation your friends are similar to your mother and possibly mother-in-law. Only tell them about your decision when

QUICK STEPS TO DEAL WITH MOTHERS

- Figure out your financial and logistical game plan before you talk to your mother. Check out Chapter 2: Feathering the Nest for specifics on how to plan. There's no point in upsetting her for no reason. Find out if it's even possible for you to stay home first.
- Distill down into a couple sentences why you feel it's important to stay home. She'll respond when you speak from the heart.
- Tell her in an unstressful time. Holidays probably aren't the best moments to break the news to your mother, especially if she's in charge of cooking a dinner for twenty family members.
- Make sure you have a plausible out. Have a ready-made excuse to get off the phone or leave the house if the conversation doesn't go well.
- Remember she's your (or your husband's) mother. You have years to prove her wrong.

you have all the answers. You can test out the idea while you're thinking about it with one or two of your closest friends. Beware. If they're going through a similar thing, they may be arguing their own issues rather than yours. Or worse, if they don't have kids, they don't understand what the big deal is. They think, "I juggle my dog and work. What's the big deal?" You may even hear lines like "Having a baby is just like raising a puppy." Take a deep breath and know that you were as insensitive to your friends when they were having babies and you were the childless chick.

Simple things to do with friends:

- Don't talk about the pregnancy and motherhood non-stop with your childless friends. They'll feel like you're talking about a club in which they're not a member.
- Pick one or two friends to really unload with about how hard everything is. Rant for an hour and get it out of your system.
- Don't make this rant a set piece of dinner conversation.
- Always ask about what's going on in your friends' lives and really listen to the answers. The world doesn't revolve around you because you're pregnant.
- If you already have children and are leaving work having actually tried to balance work and family, describe to your friends the challenges you've faced trying to manage everything and let them know how excited you are to have the opportunity to finally totally be there for your kids. Genuine friends will share your happiness.

4
Money and Power

Constructing a New Life
on the Home Front

We are positive that your husband is a loving and considerate man. Under normal circumstances, he listens or pretends he's listening to you and agrees with most of what you're saying or at most disagrees until something good comes on TV.

These aren't normal circumstances. Transitioning from working to staying home to going back to work brings volcanic eruptions of conflict and simmering resentment. You're not always going to like your husband. At times he's going to be a downright red-faced brat. Though in all fairness, there will be times he can say the same for you.

STAYING AT HOME

Things change when you stay at home. A lot of the shifts are small.

Your husband will look appraisingly at the cleanliness of the house. Is there dust on the floor? Is the garbage full? What have you been doing all day?

You will feel antsy about dirty dishes in the sink. You'll wonder if you should do more laundry. You'll ask your husband for help vacuuming on a Sunday afternoon and he'll say he's too tired from work.

You'll think, "Hey, I'm not your domestic." You'll think this isn't what you signed on for and what about that equal rights thing. But then again, you're the one who's at home more, you're not making money, and you want to be helpful. In short, you'll be conflicted.

You'll frantically rack your brain for something interesting to say in response to your husband's comments on million-dollar deals, pressing legislation, or the mean cow in the office. You have no deals, legislation, or even an office.

MONEY—SOLE BREADWINNER

Anything dealing with money is uncomfortable to discuss. Just the mention of money is enough provocation to send most people into cold sweats, prompt stomach pain, or at least an eye roll, and sense of approaching doom. We know we feel that way whenever someone mentions how much we should've saved for retirement by now versus how much we actually have saved—we curse Nordstrom and its shoe department. We aren't the millionaires next door.

We're preparing you because even the most mild-mannered husband goes through severe growing pains once it truly sinks in that he's the sole breadwinner. There's not another paycheck coming. No last-minute financial boon, unless you win the lottery.

His check is it. In the dozens of surveys we've seen and interviews we've conducted, most men don't want or expect to be the sole earner.

Most men think that the enlightened, liberated, high-powered women they married will be their financial equals. A few are aware that their wives want to stay home, but they think that's talk not reality, like when you say you're going to learn French. Even if they expect and encourage you to stay home, they still will freak out.

Let us explain.

Until now, your husband has never been financially responsible for anyone except himself. Most likely throughout dating and marriage you've been an accomplished earner, at times even making more than him. He's used to this dynamic.

He's had a lot of discretionary income. On a whim, he could plunk down the cash for a plasma screen TV or a Barcalounger. In a sense this financial independence is his last vestige of singledom and frat-like youth. He's never had to say "I have to check with the wife on that one."

Most men will fight like terriers to maintain that remnant of youth and freedom. It doesn't matter whether or not you both agreed that you would stay home with the children far before you had children. It's not a factor.

His fear of middle-age paunch, receding hairlines, and becoming like his dad is overwhelming. It's visceral, not intellectual. He doesn't want to grow up and have the responsibility of a whole family resting on his shoulders.

Sean, husband of a stay-at-home mom, said most women have no idea what kind of stress and pressure men go through being the only moneymaker—single mothers excluded.

"Most women go from being supported by their parents to supporting themselves for a few years to having their husbands support them. They've never had to say, 'If I lose my job two other people will suffer,' " Sean said.

He has spent several nights awake plotting his career path, worrying about losing his clients, and praying his bonus that year will be enough to cover the family vacation.

"I'm positive my wife has never lost a wink of sleep over any of that. She thinks everything will work out. She has a childish perception of reality," he said. "She has no idea, honestly no idea, what I deal with on a day to day basis."

It gets to him.

Jeff told us it bothered him that his wife said she knew he'd get the job he interviewed for because he's so good. He said on the surface this sounded like a compliment but underneath he felt like she didn't appreciate the work that went into getting the job, developing the contacts, or trying to make so much money. She made it sound like what he did was child's play.

These men and many others harbor resentment over being the sole breadwinners and the perception that they're not being appreciated for it. That resentment creeps into their attitudes toward their wives and into almost everything they do.

Alan won't let his wife handle their finances because she's not earning the money so he doesn't feel she understands it. Plus, he says she buys silly things like fancy dish detergent and she doesn't negotiate their insurance rates like he does. Rod says he doesn't value his wife's advice about work because she has not been out in the work world for years. He'll usually wave her off when she starts to offer her opinion about something he should do in the office.

Before you attempt to track down the aforementioned men and introduce them to the concept of equality, remember we asked these guys to give us the unvarnished truth and we can assure you they're not the only ones who think this way.

You probably feel the lack of respect emanating from your husband on occasion. But you wave it off and say to yourself it's because he's stressed and that's part of it. It's the other part that's the real problem.

If you get a man drunk enough or comfortable enough with you, nine times out of ten he'll say the same thing: Why does my educated and able-bodied wife get to stay home while I earn the money?

Now that you know this resentment is simmering, what do you do about it?

Talking about your discomfort with money is a lot more healthy than repressing all those feelings until you can't hold them in anymore and one of you ends up doing something dramatic like cutting up her credit cards or throwing his golf clubs on the front lawn.

You have to work through his feelings of resentment because you don't want to feel like you're spending his money. You don't want him to feel that way either. It's both of yours, otherwise known as "our" money.

Steps for Dealing with a Husband's Resentment

- Many husbands we talked to view their wives' time at home as more of a vacation than work. Show your husband that staying home with the kids isn't all play. Mention to him what you've done during the day, for example, dishes and laundry, going to the playground and the pediatrician's office. You know, many of the things he used to do as well when you both worked. If he sees your contribution more tangibly, he may calm down.

- Acknowledge the resentment. Then slowly take him back through the decision-making process you both went thorough to establish that you'd stay home.
- Talk him through the changes you'd have to make if you went back to work right now, for example child care arrangements, domestic help, etc.
- Talk to him about what your long-term plan is. Do you intend to get a job in two, five, or ten years? Tell him what concrete things you are doing currently to keep engaged in the professional world.

This issue is going come up again and again even if you talk about it. It will surface at the oddest times like when you purchase a pair of forty dollar flip-flops and he questions whether you need them and asks why you can't get by with the five dollar drugstore variety. But if you talk about it, money resentment will come up a lot less. Reinforcement isn't only a tool to get your children to make their beds.

ASKING FOR MONEY

A mature woman should never have an allowance. You're not twelve. Your husband isn't your parent. For years you've been able to support yourself, contribute to your 401k, and pay taxes. You should be rewarded for all those achievements and the simple fact that you and your husband are partners by having an equal say in the money.

Talk to him about the household budget. Make sure you both have an understanding of what's coming in and what has to go out every month. You'll have fewer arguments if you both understand what groceries, diapers, gym membership, etc., cost. Get a joint account and two debit cards. Both of you are responsible adults and you should be able to have equal access to money.

Never get yourself in a situation like Johanna did. Her husband was so ironfisted with the money that he handed over thirty dollars each week that she could use to pay for gas, go out to lunch, and buy things the children needed like toys. The only other form of money she had was a Target charge card. She didn't have a debit card or any other credit card.

It was sad to see her for weeks on end refusing to go out to lunch, even to McDonald's, because she couldn't afford it.

Johanna finally got sick of her financial prison and started bartering with friends. She'd buy what they needed at Target on her charge card and they paid her back with cash. She used that cash to fund her weekly activities. Her husband saw the Target bills go up a couple of hundred dollars a month, but didn't say anything.

Riley is terrified of buying clothes. We mean any kind of clothes because she's afraid her husband will yell at her for being frivolous. He screamed at her five years ago when she came home with a Burberry coat. She hasn't bought a new coat since. Riley's worn that coat so many times its pockets have holes in them. Her husband sports new suits, handmade shirts, and made-to-order shoes. He has a shoemaker in London he visits twice a year. The contrast between their appearances is startling. They don't look like they live in the same tax bracket, let alone share a bedroom.

We support fiscal responsibility except when it's based on fear and rides on the back of one half of a couple. It's not his money; it's the family's money.

Hopefully you've had the discussion about an allowance. If you haven't, tell him that's not the way it's going to work. What's more important, a happy wife or all-encompassing control over your pocketbook? He needs to compromise. You're a responsible adult who can handle the family finances. You know how to add and subtract and have been doing it for years. Better yet, you now have the time and incentive to be in charge of the finances. You can take that responsibility off your husband's hands. There's also the little matter of you raising his children with no compensation, for which he should be grateful and understanding.

Most of the men we've talked to say they understand their wives' need for financial independence and most of the time they support them, but they say they want the wives to show their appreciation.

"I'd like my wife to acknowledge that she has a nice life because of what I do. If she'd married someone else who knows what she'd be doing now. I give her a comfortable life," one man said.

The clotheshorse with the shoemaker in London says that he absolutely encourages his wife to go shopping but she's not into it. He even buys her clothes on trips and picks out things at Barneys for her to try on.

This confused us, until his wife pointed out that 90 percent of the time he's fabulous about money and shopping. It's the other 10 percent of the time when he acts like a hyperactive gorilla on acid that's the problem. It's the "I make the money" syndrome, which we'll get to shortly.

BIG PURCHASES

Once you've mastered the joint account thing, you can move on to big purchases.

There are certain items that turn us all into kids in a candy store. For us, it's shoes, purses, a nicely constructed leather jacket, most sparkly jewelry, down-stuffed couches . . . the list goes on.

For men, it varies, but anything technology oriented usually gets them. They covet the newest, smallest cell phone with the most buttons. They pine for the lightest laptops. We all know how they feel about TVs. Shiny plastic is their drug.

Suffice it to say all of these things, or even one of these things, cost lots of money. We aren't going to tell you to never splurge, because that's just not possible and it's not fun. Valentine's Day without new earrings or, for the more indulgent, a Gucci purse, doesn't spell love to us.

You will have to coordinate with each other more about what you buy than you used to. For example, our friend Janine would restrain herself from any kind of splurge for at least a month when her husband went crazy on Ralph Lauren clothes. He has his own personal shopper at the Polo store. But the moratorium on spending goes both ways. Whenever she wins a bid on a rare Arts and Crafts piece of furniture on eBay, she announces to her husband that thereafter they're on a spending ban.

HOLIDAYS

Holidays will be the hardest adjustment for both of you. If you and your husband made about the same amount of money before you left work, the shift will be more radical for you.

When you're tightening your belt, you can't compete with the siblings. No more "Wow, I wonder how expensive that gift was." It'll be more like "Huh, she made that herself, that's interesting. I didn't know people still did macramé." Some will appreciate it, others won't. But you know that holidays aren't supposed to be about a gift-giving rat race. You'll have to drop out of it. Believe us it's liberating. To be able to say to yourself, "This is all I can afford," and not agonize over your choice of gift and how it will play to the crowd is freedom to enjoy the holiday cookies and cheese loaf.

Gabriella has become such an expert at toffee making—out of necessity—that her siblings clamor to get her gift. She only makes the toffee at Christmas and that's all she's given family members for the past five years. Wendy knits. One year she gave hand-dyed and -stitched hats. The next year she doled out socks. The year after that she distributed scarves.

"It's all in the marketing. I tell my family how I picked the yarn, why it's rare or valuable, and how I dyed it. They appreciate the effort," she said.

The year Maya quit work she initiated a secret Santa rule, where each family member was given a name of one person to buy a gift for and a dollar limit.

"My sisters thanked me for doing that. It was getting ridiculous how many presents we had to buy with nieces and nephews," she said.

CUTTING BACK IN GENERAL

One girlfriend handed her husband a bag lunch on the first day she stayed home, and he laughed. He thought she was joking when she told him he had to bring his lunch. Another friend had to tell her husband they couldn't afford the new thousand-dollar suit he just bought. She offered to take it back for him so he wouldn't have to deal with the embarrassment but he said he would. The suit sat in the trunk of his car for a week before she snuck it out and returned it. For him returning the suit was a mental barrier he couldn't force himself to leap over.

A lot of guys view it as part of the macho imperative that they be able to spend whatever they want. It makes them look incredibly successful and therefore masculine in their minds.

Be gentle with your husband and yourself at first. This is a painful adjustment for both of you.

I BRING HOME THE BACON

Talking to your husband about his spending when it's technically "his" money (in only the most legalistic way) is a touchy subject. It's especially difficult when he yells back things like "I make the money, what do you do?" or "This is what relaxes me. It makes me feel good."

But you have to do it. If you don't and he's spending money like he's Donald Trump, the debt is going to build up to the point where you are irrationally mad most of the time and he maxes out your credit cards.

Start off the conversation when he's in a good mood and relaxed. Don't accuse. Don't start off with sarcasm.

If he doesn't handle it well and starts yelling, don't match his tone.

There are times in a marriage, as in parenthood, when it's best to take a deep breath and a step back before you proceed. This is definitely one of them.

It took one of our friends' breath away when her husband yelled, "How much money do you make? That's right, I make the money." Julie says she looked at her husband for a long time after he told her that he made the money. She says it was a side to her husband she didn't know was there.

She waited until he was done with his rant. More accurately, he stopped yelling when he noticed she was sitting quietly watching him.

Few things can unsettle a husband's self-confidence like an unnaturally calm wife.

He stood there for a few moments, mentally going through what he had said. When he replayed the bit about "his" money, he visibly winced. He never meant to say it, but he meant it. Today's husbands never expected to support their wives as well as their children. When they were competing with us in school and for starter jobs, it didn't cross their minds that in a few years they'd be paying for our health insurance.

YOU'RE NOT THE WOMAN
I MARRIED

This is something all men think. They may not admit it to you or in public, but when you're still in your pajamas at the end of the day the thought flashes across his brain. He remembers the sleek, manicured woman who used to wear heels and lipstick and smell nice. He reminisces about the beginning of your relationship when there were no kids and you could spend Sundays in bed reading the paper.

He also misses the woman who made money. The woman who suggested going on impromptu ski trips and paid for them.

Every so often Mariel's husband mentions to her that she's not the ambitious woman he thought he married. He'll launch into a speech about how he thought he was getting a woman bent on making partner at a white-shoe law firm by the time she was thirty-five. A woman who loved winning so much she cheated at Monopoly. Now he's married to a thirty-nine-year-old whose most ambitious moment of the day involves potty training. There was nothing in his thought process to prepare him for the sneaker-wearing woman she became.

This is a major readjustment for most men. It's going to take a long time for your husband to fully understand the value of you staying home. You should leave him home alone with the children for a day from time to time so he knows what you're going through. After five hours alone with his own children, he'll be singing your praises. He might even give you occasional backrubs and nod his head in amazement at how you handle the kids.

"SHE KEEPS TELLING ME HOW HARD IT IS"

Child-rearing is a hard job according to most women and they don't think their husbands appreciate the fact. We ran this by a few men and got a surprising response. They rolled their eyes and bitter little smiles crackled on their lips. Their whole being said, "Here we go again." We were taken aback. Doesn't everyone agree staying at home with the kids is like the hardest job out there? We became a little more timid.

"Um, don't you think what your wife is doing is hard?" we asked, knowing the phrasing wasn't the picture of impartiality.

"I hear it's the hardest job out there from her, from her friends, from the TV, even from my own children. It's a giant media campaign," one man said. "I get that it's grueling. It's grueling to work seventy hours a week too. I think my wife should shut up and deal with it."

Another man said his wife was fine, even perfect, until she got around the other hens—stay-at-home moms. They brainwashed her. They made her believe what she was doing was some kind of Herculean sacrifice. He says they ruined her.

"I think my wife should recognize that she's lucky, not many women get the opportunity to stay home and have a nice life," he said. "I bet more than half the mothers in this country would kill to be in her position."

FINDING COMMON GROUND

You used to be able to talk to your husband about work. The two of you could commiserate about micro-managing bosses and bumbling coworkers. The common ground has shrunk. You have the kids, the house, and other hobbies to talk about. Who has time for other hobbies?

Tamara reads advertising trade journals to keep up with what's happening in her husband's work life. They discuss the latest ad campaigns, what company is on the hunt to acquire another one, and what ad agencies won awards recently. Tamara said it makes her use her brain more. When she decided to go back to work, she even looked into advertising. She decided not to go into it as a profession. She became a teacher. But she still reads the advertising trades, partly because she's interested in the industry and partly because she wants to keep current with her husband.

Another friend took up golf because her husband loved the game. She got so good at it that his friends insisted he bring her along to play. She was a ringer. On business trips at luxury resorts she was out on the golf course with her husband instead of in the spa with the other wives. Consider that golf is a three- to four-hour game with lots of uninterrupted time to talk. The couple bonded and she gained another topic to talk to the guys about at office events.

Monica's sister and her husband bought a boat. They enjoy using it as a family as well as for entertaining her husband's coworkers.

When Tricia's husband decided he wanted to start a small business on the side and run it from their home, Tricia was enthusiastic and supportive. They saw it as something they could do together someday when he retired from his engineering job. In the meantime, while her husband still worked, Tricia maintained the day-to-day operations of the business out of their home while taking care of the kids.

It's important to make sure you have more than the kids in common because eventually they move out and then all you're left talking about is what's for dinner.

DON'T DO DISHES

When you worked, you and your husband shared more of the housework than you will when you stay home. Notice, we don't say you previously split the work fifty-fifty because we live in reality.

Fair or not, you'll be expected to do the majority of the housework. That means you'll be washing the dishes, making the meals, and doing the laundry.

We have found this to be a very hard adjustment. Many of our friends, and ourselves included, don't know how to cook. Sure, we can open some cans and mix things together. We probably can make five dishes between us. Mac and cheese and spaghetti are a far cry from cooking.

It becomes a little daunting to think that you are now responsible for making dinner most nights of the year because in addition to staying home, you're also trying to conserve money and you have children, which means not going out to eat as much. When you do go out, it's to a family-friendly restaurant with food-caked walls and stray crayons sticking out of bench seats.

COOKBOOKS FOR THOSE OF US WHO DON'T COOK

Fix-It and Forget-It Cookbook: Feasting with Your Slow Cooker by Dawn J. Ranck

Fix-It and Forget-It Lightly: Healthy Low-Fat Recipes for Your Slow Cooker by Phyllis Pellman Good

Mable Hoffman's Crockery Cookery, Revised Edition by Mable Hoffman

American Heart Association Quick and Easy Cookbook: More Than 200 Healthful Recipes You Can Make in Minutes American Heart Association

Betty Crocker 4-Ingredient Dinners edited by Betty Crocker

The One-Armed Cook: Quick and Easy Recipes, Smart Meal Plans, and Savvy Advice for New (and Not-So-New) Moms by Cynthia Stevens Graubart and Catherine Fliegel

Other mothers can help you. High-end grocery stores in most areas offer inexpensive cooking classes. Some cookbooks and magazines like *Everyday Food* really are accessible and easy to follow. A few even offer recipes for dishes using five ingredients or less. Follow the directions and you'll be fine. When all else fails, order pizza.

To save money and time, organize your meals in advance. Plan a week's worth of menus at the beginning of the week and set aside just one day a week for grocery shopping. By organizing like this, you can avoid multiple trips to the store. Developing this habit will not only help you while you're at home, but will free up your time when you return to work.

Another issue is that we don't know how to keep a clean house in the sense our mothers did. By the time we took home economics it was a joke. It was one of the things that boosted your average, but didn't require homework. Throughout our adult lives, we've worked and thought of cleaning as throwing everything in the laundry hamper before guests come over.

Cleaning isn't our forte. We're telling you that if you're one of the lucky ones with the cleaning gene and find scrubbing and vacuuming therapeutic, more power to you; if not, don't worry about it. If your husband complains that he misses the clean floors that the maid used to provide, tell him to look at his children and be thankful. Tell him he can mop the floors if he's in withdrawal.

Keep in mind that people forgive a multitude of sins when you have small children. On the scale of important things in life, having a clean house is low on the list compared to raising well-adjusted children. You have years to master the cleaning thing.

TIPS ON CLEANING WITHOUT REALLY CLEANING

- Be organized. Purchase a weekly planner and detail exactly what you'll do each day.
- List your cleaning chores. Some women like to devote one full day to cleaning. Others like to spread the work out over the week. For example, you could clean all the bathrooms on Monday and vacuum on Tuesday.
- If you have children old enough to take on the task, assign them cleaning chores. Since he was tall enough to reach the kitchen sink on a stool, Monica's son, Chase, would take helping with the dishwashing over playing with a toy any day.

5
Backlash

Handling Family, Friends,
and Angry Strangers

Before you gave birth 50 percent or more of your identity was wrapped up in your career. You are what you do in our society. Think about it, what's the second question most people ask you at a cocktail party? That's right, the ubiquitous What do you do?

Aside from the finances, one of the hardest adjustments to make when staying at home is ego related. Who are you without your career?

Our friends were the people we worked with. Our conversations used to be peppered with what we did at the job that day. When we described ourselves we said, "I'm a married doctor/ lawyer/accountant from New York." One of our main identifiers has been ripped away, leaving a big blank where our career used to be.

We worked hard to get to where we are. We went to school for years. We struggled up the corporate ladder and spent seventy hours or more a week in the office. We're accomplished and we take pride in the effort we put in to get us where we are.

That's why we experience a process akin to mourning when we lose that part of us. We don't know what to fill that hole in our identity with. The role of mother makes up some of it. But we have to keep something that's all ours. For some of us that means a part-time job. For others that means volunteering for something that has nothing to do with elementary school. A few of us find solace in going to school ourselves and enroll in some college classes. Others become über mothers and do everything, including making baby food from scratch.

Figuring out how to adapt to your new identity is tough on its own, but add to it public displays of ignorance and you're dealing with emotional slaps in the face on a regular basis.

How do you tell someone at a cocktail party your whole work history or who you used to be in a couple sentences?

They usually tune out after your first sentence, which is "I'm a stay-at-home mom now."

The women we've talked to have been there. They've watched as the glaze descended over people's eyes. Their attention wandered. They no longer looked at the women's faces. They look beyond, above, and around. Then there was a quick turn of their bodies as they tried to escape what they imagined would be an unending diatribe on the virtues of cloth diapers over disposable or vice versa. They think stay-at-home mothers are a conversational black hole. They think "unemployed" moms have nothing to add to their knowledge or contacts and will suck time and energy out of them.

It's hard when people gravitate toward your husband and literally turn their backs on you in conversations. Especially when you used to be equals in cocktail talk. Then, when you correct the behavior and nudge your way back into the conversation circle, it takes five minutes, tops, for them to turn their backs on you again.

We've all been brushed aside as our husband trades business cards. We've all felt like we would've had more fun if we waited in the car or stayed home with the kids. Just about everyone has had to bite their lip as a drunken older man asked why they even went to school if they were going to stay home. We've felt like blind dates at frat parties.

It shouldn't be that way. Everyone should feel comfortable and enjoy adult conversation—and not just with other mothers. We know it and you know it. Now we have to get all those clueless networkers to know it.

HOW TO MAKE THE BEST OF THOSE AWKWARD SOCIAL SITUATIONS

- Find the quiet person in the room. Talk to him or her and you'll make a friend for life.
- Ask people about themselves; even the most cold-blooded networker will stop for a few minutes and talk about ... himself.
- Remember these people aren't family. You don't have to see them for years to come.
- Remind yourself you're a smart person. Think of it like a mantra during the social situation.
- Reward yourself with cake or something equally delicious. If you promise yourself the reward before the evening begins, the whole scene becomes more manageable.

FILLING OUT FORMS

This is where it hit Monica that she was no longer considered a "lawyer." At each new doctor's appointment, and there are a lot of new doctors when you have children, the receptionist gave her the personal information form to fill out. The first time she had to fill out a form after she quit her job she panicked when she got to the "occupation" section. There it was in black and white, a whole series of questions that no longer applied to her identity. It freaked her out. She was no longer "occupied." She wrote "N/A" in the occupation blanks on the first two forms.

But on the third form, she thought that wasn't the impression she wanted to give. She has a law degree and worked in a well-known law firm for several years. "N/A" didn't say that. Neither did "stay-at-home mother."

She decided to become a compound. She wrote "attorney/stay-at-home mom," when the form asked for her occupation and put her cell phone number down as her work contact.

She thought she was a little nutty being so focused on the form. It wasn't a test. And who looks at those forms anyway?

No one does, right? Wrong. Paula, a nurse at an OB-GYN's office, said she always looks. She confesses that before she had kids when she saw "stay-at-home mom" written in the blank by occupation she treated the patient with a little less respect because she didn't think the mom was really working.

"When I used to read 'housewife' or 'stay-at-home mom' on a form, I used to think they were just a bunch of women running car pools all day," she said.

Now that she has kids she says she has a different perspective, but there are plenty of childless women and men who are looking at those forms who don't understand how sensitive we are about our new employment status.

Monica had what she perceived as a run-in with a guy at an electronics store about her answers on a form.

She was buying a digital camera for her husband as a Christmas present. The store screened anyone who wrote a check. The process involved filling out a long form, which included questions about occupation. Monica penciled in "attorney/stay-at-home mom" as usual in the blank asking for employment status.

"Where do you work?" the guy behind the counter asked.

"I don't right now," she fumbled. "I'm an attorney, but I had a baby recently and decided to become a stay-at-home mom."

"Oh, so you're unemployed," he replied in a tone that suggested caring for your children equaled watching soap operas all day.

He might as well have said, "You're fat, lady" or "You're the ugliest woman who ever walked in here." Monica felt like crying. The guy didn't even notice. He had no idea the inner turmoil Monica had boiling up inside her. He obviously didn't have a wife staying at home.

Before you tear someone's head off for being an insensitive clod, keep in mind that some people judge you and some don't. Some are clueless like the electronics store guy. Others are nasty judgers who we shake our heads at and say to ourselves, "Wait until they have children."

You're not going to know who is and who isn't judging you because you are too emotionally involved. It's prudent to assume the best of everyone and get on with your life. What the nurse in the doctor's office or the electronics store cashier thinks of you doesn't define you.

SO YOU USED TO BE A DOCTOR?

People won't say this to your face but lots of them resent the fact that you took up valuable slots in school and in the work world to build a career you've abandoned. They think you're a prima donna. They suspect you have a naïve Mary Sunshine viewpoint of the world and predict that your husband will leave you jobless and penniless in a few years for his assistant. In their imagination, they'll be able to smugly say, "I told you so." Men, especially, resent you for taking positions others, especially men, could've gotten. Whenever you look tired or have a complaint about staying at home, these people think, "What a wimp! Other women work and raise children."

Criticism of your career decision can come up when you least expect it. Donna relayed a recent experience at the doctor's office. Doctors' offices are minefields for the stay-at-home mom's ego.

Donna was there to get her blood pressure checked. Because her regular physician was off that day, a new female associate examined her.

"So what do you do?" the doctor asked, seemingly making small talk.

"I do a little part-time accounting work for my brother-in-law," Donna replied.

"Anything else?" the doctor asked as she strapped the blood pressure cuff on Donna's arm.

"Well, I stay home with my daughter," Donna answered going into female defensive mode. "Altogether, I think I have a full-time job."

Donna could sense that the doctor wasn't impressed, so she decided to share a bit more personal information she was sure would please her physician.

"You'll never believe this," Donna started with a laugh, "but in my previous life I was a research scientist for ten years. I have a PhD in physiology specializing in proteins affecting the heart muscle."

As the words left Donna's lips she sensed that the doctor was not impressed. In fact, she appeared furious. She roughly ripped the blood pressure cuff off of Donna's arm. For a split second, Donna feared that the doctor might be thinking about putting the cuff around her neck.

"I can't believe you're wasting your education," the doctor spit out.

Donna didn't know how to respond. She diffused the situation the best she could by mumbling something about tough decisions and kids, glad that the doctor took her blood pressure before the conversation became heated.

"I couldn't believe it," Donna told us. "I went there to get my blood pressure checked and change some medicine. I didn't go there for career counseling or a guilt trip."

Now you know. This is what you're up against: lots of resentment and hostility. There are people waiting for you to fail and if you do many of them will be there to comfort you in ways that will leave you feeling like you need to shower: "It's okay. This type of thing usually doesn't work out."

Who are these people? That's the tricky thing. They could be anyone. Your mother, mother-in-law, boss, old mentor, best friend, tennis partner, etc., could have a vested interest in seeing you fail. Perhaps your mother worked and raised you and she feels like your need to stay home is a comment on her mothering skills not being up to snuff. Ditto your mother-in-law. Maybe your boss didn't have kids and deeply resents other women who do because they can't tough it out in the workplace. Maybe your mentor isn't a fan of affirmative action and views you as one of the repercussions of it. Your best friend could be a new mother or doesn't have kids yet and doesn't understand why they are rearranging your life. Perhaps your tennis partner has always been a stay-at-home mom and she doesn't support going into and out of the workforce.

You have to think about other people's motivations and how they play into how they react to you. It's not all about you. It's also about their own internal struggles and issues.

When someone acts hostile toward you over what they view as you wasting your degree or ruining your child's life, figure out what else is going on. They probably have some baggage that you can help them unpack if you talk to them frankly about the issue.

You should also look carefully at who you're dealing with. If it's your mother, sister, or mother-in-law, that's one thing. If it's the teller at the bank or the dental assistant, that's something else entirely.

As one psychologist told us, "There are certain people you can easily dismiss and let them have their own opinion."

If it's a person whose opinion you value, start by trying to discern how much they're willing to even hear you. Their opinion may be set in stone and driven by factors entirely out of your control. For example, they may be secretly jealous of what you're doing and wish they could do it too. Or they could hold a firm belief that if you're not working you're freeloading and no amount of persuasive argument on your part is going to change that opinion.

Success in changing their ideas will come in large part from you. If you feel comfortable with the fact that you're staying at home, you'll be able to respond with confidence. You can honestly share with them how happy you are in your new role and how your kids love it. On the other hand, if you secretly harbor self-doubt about your decision or have your own personal belief

that most stay-at-home moms are indeed freeloaders, that senti-
ment will come through too.

Many times you'll find that no matter what you say or who
you're talking to it won't have any effect. What do you do then?

The best advice is to do nothing. Don't argue, cry, or vow
never to speak to or visit that person again. Instead, simply say, "I
respectfully disagree, but I understand," and leave it at that.

Jane shared an experience she had at a dinner party where an
older male doctor went on a ten-minute tirade about female doctors. He resented women getting into medical school, graduating,
completing residencies and internships, and then never practicing
because they have children. He fumed that at least half the
women who go to medical school don't work. He ranted and
ranted until the circle of people in the room was quiet. It was
an awkward dinner. Jane learned to walk the other way whenever
she saw the doctor headed in her direction for the rest of the
evening.

A few weeks later she learned that the doctor worked for a female doctor and the relationship wasn't a good one. Perhaps his
philosophy on women entering medical school had a connection
with this relationship. You never know what's going on with the
other person.

Though, in fairness to the intolerant doctor, we must admit
we do have a couple of friends who became pregnant in their residencies, proceeded to have children, and haven't been back to
work since. It's been years. We also did an informal poll of the
women who were on the law review with Monica in law school.
The majority of them are staying home with their children. There
is some truth to the argument that these women aren't using their
training.

But Nicky, a businesswoman with an MBA and a stay-at-
home mom, pointed out that at the time she went to business

school she wasn't married and didn't know if or when she would be, so she needed a way to earn a living. She also points out that if she married someone different she might not have had the choice to quit working. Plus, she plans on going back to work and using her degree in a few years.

Women shouldn't be denied a way to make a living because they may decide at some later date to take a few years off. As most of our girlfriends say to us, yeah they're taking five or ten years off now but they're going to go back to work and they'll be working well into their sixties, God willing, into their seventies. They say this is their retirement. They also say only a man would devise a normal career trajectory of fifty years of working with no time off.

YOU STILL DON'T KNOW HOW TO MAKE COOKIES FROM SCRATCH

There's another kind of discrimination that the former working mother is vulnerable to.

There's a tribe of women out there known as the Martha Stewarts on steroids. They try so hard to outdo one another that they end up staying up all night to create a diorama made from toothpicks and tinfoil. They look at you scornfully when you bring homemade chocolate chip cookies to the school bake sale instead of individual crème brulees with sugar caramelized by a mini blowtorch.

Don't keep up with the Marthas. Keep up with yourself. Your children will not in any way be scarred from your inability to use a mini blowtorch. You might get physically scarred if you try to learn how to use one.

We found over and over again this paradox among neo–working moms. They all had the self-confidence to risk their careers to spend time with their kids, yet they frequently suffered from bouts of self-doubt inside their new peer group, as though expertise on crème brulee or dioramas were a surrogate ego.

Monica went through this when she began staying home. Since she wasn't quite sure of the protocol among the stay-at-home moms, she tended to overdo everything. For her son's birthday parties, for example, she ordered professionally printed invitations and handed out basketballs and miniature football helmets as party favors. The low point came during her son's third-grade class's Valentine's party. The party planning committee assigned Monica the job of purchasing cups for the party. Monica was on her way to the party store to order specially engraved party cups when her mother set up an intervention for her. She explained that no one, not one child in the class, would know or care whether those cups were engraved or not. Monica snapped out of it. She's now resolved to simply be herself and not worry about keeping up with anyone else.

THE OFFICE CHRISTMAS PARTY

It comes around every year and so does the dread for many women. This is the time of year that lots of us get dressed up so we can feel inadequate for hours on end. We thought we left that level of social awkwardness behind us along with the braces and training bras.

Women have told us a myriad of horror stories. One was cornered by a coworker of her husband's who told her about all the young women he slept with since his divorce. He described his pick-up strategy in detail, which involved late night drinking and leaving his Porsche key visibly on the bar. He said the "ladies" really responded to that. Yeah, he was the kind of guy who used phrases like "the ladies."

Serena was given a drink and ushered to a corner of the room where the wives were congregating. She said it felt like segregation of the sexes. She stayed in the corner of the room all night with the rest of the women until her husband came to pick her up. It was wife night care.

When Hattie tried to talk about business with her husband's coworkers, one of them laughed, put his hand on her shoulder, and said, "Sweetie, it's okay. Let's get you another drink." He led her toward the bar and went back to his conversation. She was in a conversation time-out.

Yet another woman was accidentally locked out of the party and on the patio for most of the night. Fortunately, the Christmas party was in Houston and it was unusually warm that year. But for your absence not to be noticed for an hour is a little hurtful.

The ultimate bad party incident happened to one of the brightest women we know. Miriam was talking with a woman at the event when the subject of colleges came up. When Miriam mentioned that she held two degrees from Stanford, the other woman looked stunned and nearly dropped her drink. She searched for something to say.

"Oh, you used to be smart" was all she could think of. The conversation ended shortly after that.

Let's not forget the clothes comments. For the past few months, the most fancy thing you've put on is a pair of jeans. You have no idea what to wear. You pull a dress out of your closet that has always been a tried and true friend for you. It makes you feel pretty good, real skinny. As soon as you step into the party you notice no one else is dressed like you. It's one of those moments where you pray you can keep your coat on and not look weird for doing so. But you can't and almost the moment you check your coat another woman says something like, "What a quaint outfit" or "Don't listen to what anyone else says. I love your style. It's unique." It hurts.

Even if your outfit is appropriate it may not be the pinnacle of style. We have folded our arms over our shirts and retreated into the corner of the room as we watched other, more fashionable women float by. We imagine their more glamorous lives and instantly feel inferior.

We've prepared you for some of the bad things that may befall you at the office Christmas party. Now let's help you with some defensive action.

A week before the party, start studying up. One woman reads *Newsweek*, listens to NPR, and has CNN on in the background at home most days. She says she's one of the most informed people she knows. All that knowledge helps her make small talk at parties.

Serena reads advertising trade journals. She can talk industry trends with the best of them.

The day of the event arrange for your mother or friend to look after the kids. Make an appointment to get your hair done. Have it done the day of the party so your great blow out doesn't go to waste. At the same time, make an appointment for a manicure and pedicure.

If you want to spring for a facial too make sure you get it done a couple days before the big event so any redness you have will fade.

Start shopping for a dress a week in advance. Are we suggesting buying a new dress for the event? Yeah, we most definitely are because if you have something you're excited about wearing it will make you more willing to go to the party. New shoes? Why not.

Get a great outfit that makes you feel young, sophisticated, and slim. Bring a girlfriend along and use her as your personal shopper. Ask the sales staff what's currently in style. Make this event something to look forward to.

If you're watching money, go to the outlet stores, shop the sales, or borrow from a friend. Many nationally known retailers have great outlets. You can find their locations by visiting their Web sites. Here are a few:

Neiman Marcus (www.neimanmarcus.com)

Saks Fifth Avenue (www.saks.com)

Nordstrom (www.nordstrom.com)

Talbots (www.talbots.com)

Ann Taylor (www.anntaylor.com)

Turn on some music that pumps you up and get ready.

Having a good day before the party is crucial to your mindset at the party. You know how it is, the night your child decides to paint the kitchen walls with spaghetti sauce is the night that you are more tense than a rubber band stretched around the Sunday paper. But the day you've had a massage, a nap, or a good hour to read, you can handle anything.

When you go to the party there's strategy as well. Whenever anyone at her husband's events asked Darlene what she did she told them she was a writer. Their eyes would brighten. It sounded so exotic to them. They would ask tons of questions. She would tell them what she was working on and they would be enraptured. What Darlene said was the truth and it wasn't.

Darlene was a stay-at-home mom who wrote in her spare time. It was her eventual goal to get something published, but she wasn't actively pursuing it. Darlene says she told people what they'd be most interested in and what they respected. Darlene used to work in public relations and she says she used her experience to help her understand her audience.

"I wanted them to view me as a peer, not someone who was hard for them to comprehend."

Kate had a different strategy. She found the other people in the room who were standing awkwardly alone, went up to them, and made conversation. She made the people feel more at ease and gave herself something to do. She says she also made many friends because the people were so grateful that someone talked to them. It was a strategy her mother used to employ whenever she went to events.

One more piece of advice—never drink more than two glasses of wine at an office Christmas party. We know everyone else is drinking more, but they work there. They have more leeway than you do. They have next Monday and every work day after that to make up for their slurred impersonation of the boss. (Though even they shouldn't be slamming down the shots.)

Don't put yourself in the position of Lana. She spent a good fifteen minutes listing all the alcohol she consumed at the party and earlier in the day with the CEO and his wife. She kept repeating, "I'm so drunk." We think they noticed that before she said it. Her husband tried to pull her away from his boss but to no avail. He's still employed at the company; she doesn't go to the parties anymore.

You don't want to be tipsy. You don't want to slur. You will be mortified the next day if you remember speaking too loudly and repeating things you said. You don't want to be what everyone else remembers about the party. Your husband's colleagues may serve as future networking partners or mentors when you want to go back to work.

BEWARE THE SELF-INFLICTED IDENTITY CRISIS

We've talked a lot about the impact others can have on your ego as you move from working woman to stay-at-home mom. Now let's talk about you. In making the transition, can you become your own worst enemy? This is important because your success in returning to work will depend in large part on your confidence in your next job search. Don't become a shadow of your former professional self because your ability to project confidence to a prospective employer will suffer.

Areas to Watch Out For

- Sweats aren't a uniform. There's no mom handbook that mandates mothers must wear shape-obscuring, badly mismatched cotton clothing or a shirt with an appliqué of a flower on it. Keep up with the latest fashions, so that the day you do decide to return to work you will have more important things to think about than what to wear.
- Remember the "freshman ten" when you entered college? Well, the same thing can happen when you stay at home with the children. At lunch, you order yourself a salad with fat-free dressing and your child a cheeseburger and French fries. Being a small child, finicky in her eating habits, she barely eats a bite. Nevertheless, when the meal is over, every morsel of food is gone. Where did it all go? You ate it. You get the picture.

Food is without a doubt one of the biggest pitfalls to becoming a stay-at-home mom. When you decide to return to work, you don't want to have to add "drop thirty pounds" to your to-do list.

• Hanging out solely with other stay-at-home moms. Make the extra effort to maintain contacts with friends who work. Get a babysitter, dress up, and meet them for cocktails occasionally. It gets you out of your comfort zone.

CEO Mom Syndrome

There is another self-defeating behavior to watch out for when you become a stay-at-home mom. We call it CEO Mom syndrome. It arises when you have an epiphany that if you can't be CEO of a Fortune 500 company because you put your career on hold, perhaps you should nurture junior to the top spot.

Monica knows CEO Mom syndrome all too well. As soon as she didn't have a staff to give direction to she began monitoring her son Jared's homework assignments and critiquing his projects and reports. She invested at least half her daily energy into educating Jared. She bought every workbook and program she could find in almost every subject imaginable and worked daily with him at the kitchen table. When she and her husband were looking at kindergartens in Washington, D.C., and it looked like Jared might be behind, she doubled her efforts and spent five hundred dollars on a math program. She created an incentive system where Jared would earn points for each page of any workbook he completed. By finishing a predetermined number of points, he could earn toys and games he wanted. Her system worked so well that by the end of kindergarten, he was reading well and had more toys than would fit in his room.

In second grade, he expressed an interest in learning multiplication because a couple friends were taught how to do it over the summer by overachieving parents. When we say "an interest," let's just say he might have mentioned it in passing one day. Monica jumped on it. She hired a tutor to instruct him once a week for the entire school year to help him to master the multiplication table. His second-grade teacher wasn't real enthusiastic. Jared was a straight-A student and already excelling in math; hiring a tutor seemed to be overkill.

Monica finally got the message when she threatened to take away Jared's video games because she thought his grades were slipping from A's to A minuses. He was near tears when it clicked for Monica that she was punishing her son for being an A-minus student. Most parents would give their children ice cream for such a feat.

Jared is now a fourth grader and remains a straight-A student. Monica makes sure he gets his homework done and keeps up with his projects, but she is reformed . . . okay, she's trying. She bites her tongue when he proudly leaves home with a class project that looks like, well, like a child made it.

You know how a kid draws three blue scribbles on the top of the page to suggest a blue sky? In the old days, Monica made Jared sit there and neatly color it all in. Each time he had a project to turn in she gave him coloring lessons. Now, she just lets him take it to school, and he still gets good grades.

Monica's initial response to her son's academic activities upon her departure from the workplace is typical. Another reformed professional mother we know bought all workbooks and teaching aids she could find and set up workstations in her car so that her children could be learning no matter where they went. She had two clipboards, two binders with various types of paper, two pencil holders with pencils, tape, crayons, erasers, and glue sticks, and an expandable folder with activity booklets.

Why is this a problem?

First, it places incredible pressure on your child. As Dr. Hellen Streicher, a child psychologist, told us, "When you set the bar so high for your child, you are setting him up for failure. As a result, you'll oftentimes end up with a depressed and anger-prone child."

"Your children are not your coworkers. They are not your equals," says Dr. Streicher. "If you find yourself living vicariously through your child, stop and get your bearings as to where your child is. Pull yourself back and remember that this isn't corporate America, it's your child."

She notes that most times parents find themselves behaving in this manner because that's what they're accustomed to doing at work. They may even subconsciously bring the traits that made them successful in the workplace into their child rearing, but the two rarely go together. To combat this, Dr. Streicher suggests that stay-at-home moms educate themselves as much as possible about child development.

Focusing all your energy and ambition on your child is detrimental to you as well because it inhibits your ability to further your own personal and professional goals. Your time could be better spent volunteering and networking, after all it's not like your personal ambition died when you decided to stay at home. Finding more appropriate outlets for your ambition will be better for you and healthier for your child.

THE DIVISION BETWEEN STAY-AT-HOME AND WORKING MOMS

Be warned there is a sharp division between stay-at-home and working moms. Each group has its stereotypes of the other and from what we've observed neither particularly likes the other—it's been called the mommy wars.

We used to be the working mom who had a glamorous career and loads of intellectual stimulation. Admit it. We were also the ones looking down our noses at the mom in sweats with unwashed hair pushing her kids through the grocery aisles in a stroller. Part of us envied her and the other part thought, have some pride. We're the moms, whether we know it or not, who made some comment to another mom that was offensive to her. We didn't intend it, but that mom has probably told a couple other moms about our faux pas.

These stay-at-home mothers have been in the trenches together for the past few years or months. They've bonded like war veterans. They've confessed to one another their frustrations when they couldn't stop their baby's crying. They have felt snubs and slights, whether imagined or real, when they're at the grocery store pushing a mammoth cart full of string cheese and baby food jars and a woman in a business suit whisks by them with her basket full of imported cheese and wine. Most of them love their lives, but they all have a nagging need to justify their existence to some extent, which can come out in some weird ways. Monica knows—she's done it herself.

One new stay-at-home mom told us, "I woke up one day and realized I had a lot of respect for women I used to roll my eyes at."

We're preparing you for some of the coldness you may feel from other mothers when you first embark on making friends with them. It may be tough going for a while. Stick it out. Be upbeat and remember, just because you are all mothers doesn't mean you'll all get along or like one another. You have to find your circle. It may take a while, but it'll happen so don't feel depressed if you meet some resistance initially. In more ways than are comfortable, it's like high school all over again. You have to find your clique.

Don't become a stay-at-home mom snob yourself.

Stop yourself whenever you're tempted to scoff at the bag of Chips Ahoy! cookies your working mother counterpart brings to the class Valentine's party as you cart in the material for the handmade heart-shaped picture frame craft. Lower your nose about two inches, missy.

6

One Foot In, One Foot Out

How Can They Miss You If You Don't Really Go Away?

Keeping up your contacts and gaining new ones is easier than you think and an absolute necessity if you want to return to work.

Don't roll your eyes and think, Yeah, that's for the women who organize their recipes in categories and laminate them. We don't even vacuum our houses once a week but we build up contacts. You probably do too but you don't realize it.

How? We deliberately make the time in our schedules because we know that ultimately having lunch with our old boss a few times a year is more important than a clean rug. We also volunteer and do things we love like working on a political campaign and Pilates. It's surprising how far the contacts we make doing the simplest activity can take us.

It's all about keeping yourself in front of people. Don't shut down your professional side because you're staying home.

Karen Hughes sure didn't.

Karen is President George W. Bush's former counselor in the White House. She quit midway through his first term because her son wanted to go back to Austin, Texas, for his final years of high school and because she wanted to spend more time with him. She stayed at home but she did her version of it, which included writing a book, giving speeches, and serving on councils.

You'd think that taking yourself out of the White House and moving to another state would exile you from working with the administration, but Karen found a few ways to maintain a toehold. She used her interest in the women of Afghanistan to continue conversations with her contacts. She also served on the U.S.–Afghan Women's Council.

Her interest in Afghanistan ensured that her conversations with her former colleagues advanced an issue instead of rehashing old ground. It also showed she could be an asset outside of her known area of expertise, public relations.

"It's important to find something you're passionate about and keep current. If you're staying home devote one or two mornings a week to an interest of yours and develop it. Make it something that isn't attached to your children but is yours," Karen says.

That strategy turned Karen's passion for politics into a paying job and ultimately a nationally coveted political job.

She says she's never consciously networked. She's never been one of those people on the make at events. You know the guy who shakes everyone's hand, flashes a two-dollar smile and a card while scoping out what others can do for him.

Karen went into politics because she loved it. She built up a base of friends who shared the same interest. It was easy for her to keep up her contacts when she moved from job to job because she liked her contacts.

The beginning years of her political career didn't show any signs that she was White House bound. She struggled with piecemeal jobs and unglamorous assignments like handing out leaflets in parking lots.

She kept at it because she truly enjoyed what she did. In those lean years, she met regularly with a group of political people on Saturday mornings for breakfast. They hashed out problems and gave each other job leads. They grew up together professionally and now are some of the most prominent political leaders in Texas and the nation. Not a bad group of friends for a woman who hates to network.

Pam worked as a pharmaceutical sales representative and manager for more than a decade. No joke—she loved her job. She enjoyed accomplishing concrete goals and felt that she was, in an indirect way, helping people.

When her husband's job relocated him to Tennessee from Pennsylvania she had to quit. But she didn't let her contacts wither. She read trade journals and business magazines because she was still fascinated by the industry. It didn't feel like work to her. Whenever something concerning her coworkers or old bosses was in the news she e-mailed them.

"I wrote one note to the guy who used to run our division. I'd heard he'd gotten a promotion so I wrote to congratulate him. Even though I hadn't had that much contact with him directly when I was working, he responded to me," she said.

All this was useful when she put together a business plan for a company that will perform outcome studies for pharmaceutical companies. The firm will track new drugs as they enter the marketplace and follow consumer response to those drugs. Through her contacts, Pam enlisted the help of a New Mexico company to handle the database she'll need when her business is up and running. She picked her former colleagues' brains about the best way to set up the business and who to approach about contracts.

"E-mail allows you to stay in touch so easily, now there's no excuse to lose touch," she said.

Former Texas governor Ann Richards never thought she'd run for political office. She spent years volunteering for other people's campaigns because she felt passionately about the political process. A person who agrees to plant candidate signs all over town isn't in it for the career opportunities, she's doing it because she believes in something. That love of the game led to lifelong friendships and a political network that helped her run for office.

That kind of networking isn't planned or calculated. If it was you'd have to be the most patient sociopath ever created. There's no guarantee any of the networking is going to pay off. You have to commit yourself to something you love or else you'll be bitter about all the sweat equity you're putting in. You have to love the grunt work. The small jobs. The lack of regular money or not much money at all.

Monica knows finding that passion has saved her sanity many days when she felt like she was a virtual shut-in in the suburbs. She relishes the opportunity to dress up, get out of the house, and talk to people about issues not related to her children. It makes her feel independent, young, and creative. It's amazing what a throw-up free shirt and no *Sesame Street* can do for your self-esteem. Within in an hour or two of acting like a grown-up with other grown-ups, a calm assuredness comes over you that's refreshing.

FINDING YOUR PASSION WHILE NETWORKING

It's possible to discover a new interest that ultimately leads to a future job you'll truly enjoy. Here are some ideas for finding new passions.

- Think about the subjects that you can talk about for hours, go out of your way to read about, or feel happy when you're doing them. Write a list.
- From that list, pick two areas to pursue.
- Start small. Interested in yoga? Get involved in your local yoga studio. Find out about becoming an instructor. Have a thing for cooking? Sign up for a couple of classes.
- Be patient and open-minded. Watch where that interest takes you. You may find a new career or a new group of friends. Don't come in with preconceived notions of what you'll get out of it.
- Be prepared to step up when opportunities open up. Often in our interviews we asked women how they got the opportunities they did and invariably they said right place, right time. They were qualified and able to fill the need.

You may be asking, What does yoga have to do with my former career as an accountant? Maybe your new career will be yoga studio owner. Perhaps you'll meet other people through yoga who can help you jump-start your accounting career again. The point is, following your interests is another way to put yourself out there and subtly market yourself.

OFFICE PARTIES AS CAREER DEVELOPMENT

Husbands' office Christmas parties don't have a real positive reputation for good reason. You're generally surrounded by people who don't know you and don't really care to know you, but there's a way to turn it around.

Linda thought of the parties as networking opportunities for her, not just for her husband. She targeted successful women and talked to them about their careers. She mentioned her skills and the fact that she'd like to go back to work in a few years. She asked them to lunch and developed several mentors who have given her valuable career advice.

"I wasn't self-conscious at the parties because I had a clear goal I was trying to achieve," Linda says.

NETWORKING WITH OTHER STAY-AT-HOME MOMS

We know you're thinking, What can a group of stay-at-home moms do for my future career?

Always expand the network of people you know, even if it's not readily apparent how people can help you. You'll be surprised at who comes through for you in a couple years when you want to go back to work. Most of the stay-at-home moms you meet will also be going back to work in a few years as well.

Gina holds a monthly wine and appetizer feast for thirty neighborhood women. They rotate houses each month and make sure the husbands are free to provide child care. The feasts originally started as a book club but quickly evolved into a conversation club. Two hours of adult conversation without interruption sounds like heaven, doesn't it?

Skylar organizes mommy movie nights. Every two weeks a group of moms meet for dinner or appetizers and some wine and a movie. They all dress in high heels and cocktail attire. It's a great way to get out of their comfort zones and back into the adult world. It's important to extend yourself outside of the mommy identity. You are more than a mother and you need to remind yourself of that every now and then.

There are lots of book clubs out there. Ask friends if they belong to one. Call a local bookstore. Start your own.

Adele pays for a yoga teacher to come to her house and teach a class for her and her friends on weekends. It's a great way to see friends and get in shape in a nonthreatening place. You know what we mean, a place that isn't full of spandex-covered muscled bodies and mirrors.

Don't worry that you need, crave, obsess about having a group of women like this to hang out with sans children occasionally. It's normal. It doesn't make you a bad mother. If anything it makes you a sane mother and a hip woman to boot. If none of your friends have organized anything like this, do it yourself. Motherhood makes us all more inclined to organize. Follow your natural instincts. It doesn't even have to cost anything. Randy got together a group of four women to walk in the morning. They get up at 6:00 A.M. and walk for an hour. Their husbands look after the babies while they walk. Sometimes Randy and the other women even meet for an afternoon walk and bring the children. They look like a baby gang walking down the street with their strollers lined up side by side.

VOLUNTEERING

It's one of the easiest ways to get in front of a wide variety of people with a ready-made subject to talk about. You didn't have a reason to talk to the vice president of the local bank until you wanted to form an alliance for a fund raiser at your children's school or the city's museum. Volunteering gives you face time with business and community leaders. Once these people know you, they'll be more amenable to helping you when you want to go back to work.

Daphne is the hyper-achiever volunteer, and we don't mean she produces the most cookies at the school bake sale. Well, she does that too. Daphne is a smart volunteer, sort of a venture capitalist volunteer. She looks at situations that have potential for growth, meaning she doesn't rush to help the most successful biggest fund raiser with dozens of people clamoring to volunteer. She finds the events that are small and could grow with the help of her talents. In doing so, she went from event designer to financial advisor at a museum in a couple years.

Daphne speaks Spanish fluently. She offered to help run the exchange student and cultural awareness programs at her children's school. The role mushroomed into her helping parents prep for exchange students. She even gave tours to other parents who were concerned about a multicultural approach and who were looking at the school. The parents were often new to town and needed recommendations for other services. Daphne's husband is a dentist so it was a nice tie-in for new business.

When her older children's high school was casting about for a new way to raise money, Daphne saw an opportunity to take the fund raising to the next level. She took over a woodworking project and turned it into a money-making operation.

The year before a former teacher had donated old wood-carving tools to the school. The kids learned how to make rudimentary designs in the wood and made small wooden boxes that they sold in a school craft fair for twenty dollars each.

Daphne decided to make benches and tables with ceramic tile mosaic designs. She bought boxes of discontinued tiles from home goods stores and hired a professional furniture maker to supervise the students' progress. Each class was in charge of making a bench and table. After four months of hard work, she had eight pieces of furniture with beautiful designs. She had the same professional woodworker stain the legs of the benches and tables.

Daphne didn't stop there. She had the school display the pieces in the library for two weeks before the event to get parents talking. She hired a professional auctioneer to handle the bidding. They raised $21,000.

The event was such a hit that local TV stations did stories on it and the newspaper wrote an article. Daphne got nicknamed the "woods woman." The exposure gave her a reputation as a phenomenal fund raiser and opened doors. She met mothers who were plugged into the fund-raising circuit. They enlisted Daphne's help on a benefit for the Museum of Natural History.

She was named design chair for the event and given $8,000 to turn a ballroom into a Mexican-themed paradise. That budget wasn't enough to buy floral arrangements, so Daphne bought bags of dried sage flowers and pinion and scattered them on the floor. She approached a couple of vendors about letting the museum borrow things in exchange for free advertising in the museum's programs and free tickets to the events. She got large Day of the Dead skeletons and long benches for free.

She bought rolls of brightly patterned fabric for a reduced price from a store that was going out of business. She spent hundreds of hours sewing fifty pillows and wall coverings to transform the ballroom into a hip Mexican cantina. She sewed at night when her children were sleeping or on the weekends when the kids were playing.

"It was great for my kids to see me doing what I said I was going to do," Daphne said about why she worked so hard. The other reason was because the design had her name on it, so she wanted it to be wonderful.

She purchased five-dollar tin lanterns for table centerpieces.

She used the rest of her money to hire mariachi players and fortune-tellers.

The museum board was impressed, so impressed they asked her to be on the board.

When she joined the museum's board, Daphne didn't let the success go to her head. She saw herself as starting from the ground floor. She says her strategy for the first few meetings was to be quiet and learn. Daphne's big on first impressions and didn't want to put her foot in her mouth by saying something wrong. So she'd listen, absorb, and do the reading.

When the board decided to do strategic planning they gave her a whole new level of responsibility, which built her résumé and contacts. She did a lot of the number crunching and financial work for the plan. She basically served as the chief financial officer. She forecasted revenue, recalculated the price point for museum tickets, and set an ambitious goal for corporate sponsorships.

The role raised her profile enough that other boards offered her positions. The world of board membership is small. After you do well on one board, other boards want you, which is great if you can afford it.

Many boards require a commitment of $1,000 to $5,000 depending on the board and the level you're at. Several nonprofits have two-tiered boards. One is a junior level, which costs less and requires less of a time commitment than the advisory or senior board. Some boards require time commitments in lieu of money.

Often your husband's employer or your former employer contributes money to the organization and may be interested in sponsoring some or all of your board fee. It's good to investigate the cost of joining before you do.

If you don't want or can't afford to spend the money you can defer joining a board and continue to work on event committees. You'll mingle with lots of connected people and show off your skills doing the committee work.

Like Daphne, Tucker is an über volunteer but her opportunity came to her. Her ascension into that world happened almost by accident and free of charge.

Following the birth of her second child, Tucker agreed to do some pro bono strategic planning work for a local arts organization called Young Audiences (now Big Thought).

Even after she quit her job to spend more time with her children, she continued working on the organization's strategic plan. Young Audiences liked her work so much they asked her to continue to volunteer for them after the plan was completed. Eventually, she became chairman of the board and president of the organization while juggling her four children's activities.

Another dividend to choosing your volunteer activity wisely is expanding your contacts base. Arts and civic boards are comprised of men and women who are leaders in their community. These are people you could potentially turn to for job leads and advice if and when you decide to return to work.

"If I wanted to get a job right now," Tucker said, "the people I met through the board would be the people I would go to first because they have seen my effectiveness in a job setting outside the mommy setting."

Karen Hughes seconds the idea of volunteering in a smart way. Don't agree to volunteer for every child-oriented activity there is. We've said it before, but it's important to emphasize it. Look at your interests and find volunteer opportunities that revolve around them. You will be networking and enjoying it.

I KNOW I SIGNED UP FOR IT
BUT DO I HAVE TO GO?

We understand how it is when you sign up for an event. It sounds great when it's two weeks away. Then the day rolls around and you've got a million things to do or a million things you have done. You don't feel like doing it. You'll have to talk to people and be cheery. Wouldn't it be better to have quality time with your kids?

Even our über volunteer Daphne has those days when she wants to stay home instead of going to a volunteer event. It's a lot easier to keep your sweats on and eat pizza with your kids than shower, change, and run out the door. But you have to make yourself do it. We're not going to lie to you: the first couple meetings you go to will feel a little awkward. You won't know a lot of people. You aren't schooled in the ways of the group. It's been a while since you dressed up and stood around in heels. Persevere and it'll improve. The more you do it, the better you get at it.

Daphne has a few tips for going to events.

- Get to an event early so you have time to talk to lots of people before they get inundated with other friends.
- If you know dinner or appetizers will be offered, eat before you get there. You don't want to be so hungry that you're focused on food instead of meeting people. It's hard to eat, talk, and shake hands at the same time.
- When you go up for a glass of wine you can snag two glasses and offer one to someone else. It'll give you a conversation starter.
- Ask the group to assign you a mentor or buddy. The

person is usually a senior member of the organization. She knows everyone and can school you on how the group functions.

MULTITASKING

A lot of us respond with "I don't have time" when another responsibility is thrown our way. It's our knee-jerk reaction because we feel like there aren't enough hours in the day to fulfill the obligations we already have—kids, husband, house, meals, pets . . . the list goes on and on. That's why the thought of getting involved with politics or giving time to an organization sends our hearts racing.

We gossip with each other about those seeming superwomen who do everything while managing to smell nice and stay skinny. They must be addicted to their children's Ritalin. That's the only explanation we can come up with to explain their hyperactivity and productivity.

We decided to go right to the source and ask one of the superwomen we know how she does it.

Kathy serves on charitable boards, delivers Meals on Wheels, coaches her daughter's basketball team, leads the Cub Scout pack, chairs fund-raising committees at her children's school, and runs a design magazine that she and her husband purchased part time. In her "spare time" she plays tennis in a league. Did we mention she has four children?

We know what you're thinking because we think it too, there's no way any single human being can accomplish all that. Let's hear her out.

She credits her father with guiding her path.

Her father told her that there are segments to life—learning, earning, and serving. He suggested to her that if she planned carefully, she could weave in and out of these segments successfully.

"So I segment these things," she said. "I tell myself this is my time to be a good mom. This is my time to be a good volunteer."

She carefully chooses what she feels she can successfully accomplish, and she's organized about it, even going so far as to keep a huge calendar that sits on top of the kitchen counter in full view of everyone in her family. The calendar, which is the size of a small billboard, contains every aspect of her day, month, and year. It has at least ten lines per day, including margin notes and lots of white out as schedules change. No one in the family makes a move before consulting it.

The other big factors in her ability to maintain a balance that she feels comfortable with are the productivity paradigm and trading off.

We all encounter the productivity paradigm in one form or another. We could spend three hours cleaning the house, or if we're pressed by an unexpected play date or in-law visit, we could accomplish about the same amount of cleaning in one hour. Sure there's more stress, but we're more efficient. Most of us can cram things into our schedule and become more productive up to a point. At that point we become too stressed to cope and nothing gets done the way we'd like. It's a sign to cut back. What's that point? It's different for all of us.

Kathy has found hers. She says she's realistic about what she can and cannot accomplish. She sacrifices certain activities to do others. This is the other big factor in maintaining balance, realizing you can't do everything in one day or one week. Sometimes you have to put things off until tomorrow.

"I ignore my own stuff—shopping and reading," she explained. "I don't do the ladies-who-lunch thing, and I've cut back my tennis. I don't mind, though, because I feel like I get a lot from what I'm doing."

Recently, Kathy added a new role to her busy itinerary—magazine publisher. She and her husband purchased a design magazine from a woman at her child's school and grew it into a regional publishing company. For a while, her husband ran things full time. Then he was offered the position of president of another larger publishing company. Rather than give up their own firm, she and her husband decided that she should step in and run things on a part-time basis. She hasn't been doing it long, but she thinks things are going okay.

Not everyone can keep up Kathy's pace, nor would they want to. We're out on both counts. And that's the point. Kathy makes choices that work for her. She does a lot, but she's not pulling out her hair, stressing, or complaining—though most people wouldn't trade places with her.

Don't let others guide your life. If you think you can handle something and want to do it, go for it. You'll surprise yourself. Granted, you may never be like Kathy, but you may find a balance in your own life that makes the juggling act well worth your time.

FINDING THE TIME

You're probably saying to yourself right about now, "Telling me to volunteer for organizations and political campaigns sounds great, but when am I supposed to do all this when I have kids to take care of, homework to help with, meals to cook, and a house to clean? I'm barely managing as it is!"

We agree it's a daunting task, but we also know it can be done. The key is organization. You have to plan carefully and be realistic about your limitations. You also have to come to grips with the idea that sometimes, despite your best intentions and most careful planning, you'll end up flying by the seat of your pants to get certain things done or give up on doing them entirely.

First, decide what you absolutely need or have the physical ability to do. Write these items on your calendar in ink and bold letters. These are the things you must do to keep your home in order and your sanity in check.

Next, evaluate your overall family situation. If your child is a newborn, for example, your free time will be limited because caring for your baby will consume nearly every waking moment of your day. You may only be able to engage in outside activities once a week on Mom's Day Out or when your mother or sister can come over to help. If your child is in school, you may find yourself with time to take on additional outside responsibilities during school hours or you may try to arrange for set weekly child care after school or enlist your spouse's help if some of your activities occur during time your children are at home.

Finally, carefully select activities that you feel you can reasonably and successfully undertake and fit comfortably in your schedule. We say "comfortably" because if you try to cram several commitments into your limited free time, you'll end up with an ulcer or worse. In addition, you'll end up hating what you're doing and derive no benefit from it whatsoever.

You can be creative in how you handle things. Monica's friend Melissa is one of the top volunteers at her son's school. Melissa serves as a homeroom mother, Cub Scout den leader, and director of the school store among other things. She does all this while caring for her three boys ages three to ten. Melissa's husband travels out of town a lot, so she's often left to deal with the kids by herself morning to night.

When performing one of her duties, many times Melissa simply brings the boys along, finds something fun and safe they can do, and then does her volunteer work. It is not uncommon to see Melissa's car parked in the car pool line with the trunk lid up while she sells school spirit items from the back of her car. Meanwhile, her two youngest children sit and play happily in the backseat.

When Melissa realized a year ago that her Cub Scout den would need to meet during a time that her two youngest boys were out of school, she enlisted the help of a girl in middle school. Just prior to each meeting, Melissa walked her children over to the school playground where the girl would watch and

---

WAYS TO MULTITASK AND KEEP YOUR SANITY

- Carefully choose the extra activities you undertake. Are these things you're passionate about? Will they further your goals? It's important that you're doing something you truly enjoy and you feel is worthwhile because you'll be sacrificing in order to do it.
- Find good child care on the days and times you'll be engaging in these outside activities. This may mean hiring a part-time nanny, taking your child to a Mother's Day Out program, or enlisting your mother, sister, or spouse in the cause.
- Buy a calendar or develop some similar system for keeping track of your activities as well as those of the family. Have it in plain view, where the whole family can refer to it.
- Accept the fact that you will have to sacrifice some activities to do others. Your house might not be as spotless as it was before, but you'll be making valuable contacts in return.

entertain the kids until Melissa finished with the meeting. Whenever Melissa has a more involved project that she knows will take up more of her time, Melissa's mom visits from out of town and helps her take care of the kids.

You know your own circumstances and limitations. Be honest with yourself. If you are realistic about what you can and cannot do, careful planning can help you achieve your goals.

WHERE CAN YOU VOLUNTEER?

Your child's school is an excellent place to start. Many schools ask for parents' assistance in organizing fund raisers, reviewing curriculum, and developing strategic plans. By offering your time, you not only help your child, but you network with other parents who either have jobs themselves or have spouses who do. Also, among these other parents are a couple of extremely experienced volunteers who will pull you into other organizations they commit time to. They'll introduce you to the group that raises money for the ballet or the opera and overnight your social circle, and therefore your future job networking circle, will double.

Another good source of volunteer work is your city's Junior League. The only downside is you must be nominated by a current Junior League member.

VOLUNTEERING YOUR WAY INTO A PART-TIME JOB

Lucinda is a corporate lawyer who took time off but didn't want to lose all her contacts. She thought that as long as she was in front of professionals on a regular basis she'd be all right.

VOLUNTEER RESOURCES

- Hands On Network (www.handsonnetwork.org)
- Volunteer Match (www.volunteermatch.org)
- Points of Light Foundation (www.pointsoflight.org)
- *Volunteering: How Service Enriches Your Life—and How Its Unexpected Halo Effect Boosts Your Career* by John Raynolds
- *The Back Door Guide to Short-Term Job Adventures: Internships, Extraordinary Experiences, Seasonal Jobs, Volunteering, Working Abroad* by Michael Landes
- *The Busy Family's Guide to Volunteering: Doing Good Together* by Jenny Friedman

She thought about teaching a class but she didn't have a specialty area to develop a curriculum around. Instead of waiting around for the perfect situation, she decided to coach her old law school's mock trial team. She knew the dean was always short on people willing to devote the time to train young law students how to argue a case. She reasoned if she coached the team the dean would think highly of her and it would give her an excuse to stay in contact with him and old professors. Then if any opportunities came up, she'd be in a position to slip into teaching a class.

She headed the mock trial team for three years. She spent countless hours coaching students on their presentation skills and editing their briefs. The teams did very well. They advanced in national competitions and even had the opportunity to compete internationally.

Spending all that time at the school and coordinating with the administration about travel and other expenses, Lucinda did get close to the dean. When an opportunity came up to teach a class on the Americans with Disabilities Act (the ADA), he offered it to her. Right place, right time: It's good to get exposure.

Lucinda taught the class and brushed up her knowledge of the ADA. When she went back to work she was able to put a couple more lines on her résumé.

Marley used to be a journalist. For several years when she was a reporter, she lectured once a semester for an investigative journalism class at the local university. When she decided to quit to raise her children, she looked into the possibility of teaching a class at the university. They didn't have a slot available, but they asked her if she'd be interested in advising the student newspaper. She agreed and spent fifteen hours a week at the newspaper office. She advised students on interview techniques and edited stories. She perfected her teaching techniques and became a student favorite. Even people who didn't work at the paper sought out her advice. She worked there for two years before the school offered her a job teaching a class. She parlayed one class into instructing three. Now she's a full-fledged professor.

One thing both these stories show is that you can use volunteering to worm your way into teaching after you've forged a relationship with the university. If you're patient and offer your time and expertise on other projects, you will be rewarded for your efforts.

Here are some tips from Marley and Lucinda:

- Contact the division of your local university that could benefit from your skills, for example, student newspaper if you're a journalist.
- Arrange a meeting with a professor or student coordinator.
- Tell them what your skill set is, your experience, and

what times you are available. Ask if they need anyone
to help out on a volunteer basis with any of the student
organizations.

- Once you're volunteering, make it your mission to
know the dean and the professors in the department.
- Make sure to do what you say you're going to and
more. People recognize good work and dependability.
- After a few months have passed and you've developed
a track record, tell them you'd be interested in a paid
position when one becomes available.

POLITICS

We've talked to several women who parlayed their passion for
politics into careers. Karen Hughes and Ann Richards are obvious
examples.

We've also talked to women who have used their love of politics as a way to boost their careers. Monica is an example.

Monica got involved in politics to develop business for her law
firm. The firm encouraged its attorneys to become active in the
community in order to meet new clients. Volunteering for organizations evenings and weekends after working an eighty-hour
week wasn't her idea of relaxing, but she did it. She began when
she was single and then continued after she married and had a
child. As she became more involved in her various commitments
while working, she unfortunately found less and less time to
spend with her son.

In the beginning, Monica signed up for the board of the Dallas
Bar Association Environmental Law Section and volunteered for
500 Inc., a group of young professionals supporting the arts.

One night a friend of hers convinced her to attend a Young

Republicans meeting. Monica was hesitant. She was tired. She wanted to go home and sleep. She had put in her volunteer duty that week.

It was 1991. George W. Bush, the son of the then president, spoke at the meeting. As he spoke, Monica became more excited about politics. She had always had an interest. Since high school, she volunteered on campaigns and interned in two congressional offices, but as a practicing attorney she hadn't found much time for political pursuits.

At the meeting, Monica recognized the state chairman of the Young Republicans. He was a former high school classmate. Back then, he was the class clown type of guy. He never struck her as the type to do something as serious as running a political organization, but he was doing just that. He invited her to become general counsel for the state organization. Not bad for an evening's work.

She agreed, and within the next few years became in ascending order the president of the downtown Dallas chapter, state chairperson, national general counsel, co-chairperson, and finally national chairperson.

In each of the positions, Monica's networking base expanded exponentially. Soon she knew young opinion leaders from coast to coast. Those contacts helped land her an offer to work on the Bush presidential campaign. Even though she decided not to work with the administration after the election, she still gets job offers.

To keep herself in her friends' minds, Monica makes three trips to Washington, D.C., a year and schedules lunches with friends working at the White House or elsewhere in the administration. Although she is not free to travel with a political campaign for months on end like she used to, she volunteers in some capacity. Now that her youngest child, Chase, is starting preschool, Monica plans to ratchet up her political activities by volunteering in the next gubernatorial election.

This brings up an important consideration. How much time you'll have to actively stay involved in politics or other pursuits will depend on the age of your child. When she's an infant or toddler, you may find it difficult to find time to pursue networking opportunities or volunteer. You'll need to carefully plan and work out special child-care arrangements that accommodate your goals. Once your child enters preschool, however, the hours he is in school provide you the time you'll need to accomplish some of your volunteering and networking goals. As your child progresses in school, your opportunities to expand activities targeted toward your ultimate career goals also increase, at the very least, during the hours he's in school.

Our friend Shari is a stay-at-home mom but she's keeping her hand in the job market by serving on the Texas Pension Review Board. The board oversees all the Texas public pension plans, over $150 billion in assets. The group meets six times a year and allows Shari to network with members of the legislature, money managers, leaders of the community, and city employees.

Ann Richards, governor of Texas in the early nineties, was the ultimate stay-at-home mom who used her network to get a good job. Ann stayed home to raise her four children for more than a decade. The one interest she followed with zeal was politics. She volunteered for political campaigns; she stuffed envelopes and canvassed door to door for candidates. After years of licking stamps, she gained enough experience and a solid reputation to run a campaign for Sarah Weddington, the woman who argued *Roe v. Wade* in the Supreme Court, for the state legislature. Weddington won.

Soon after that Ann's friends convinced her to run for county commissioner. She won. She continued to win larger elections. Eventually she ran for governor of Texas and won.

As she spent more time in politics, she spent less time at home. She says she thinks her younger child suffered some because she couldn't devote the same amount of attention she used to at home.

"But I don't regret it," Ann says. "You can't fall into the trap of thinking you have to do it all or can do it all. You have to take advantage of opportunities when they're offered."

SPORTS

This category surprised us until the athletic among us explained it. Lucy is a passionate tennis player. She got more into it during the three years she stayed home. She joined a league at a nearby country club and started playing matches a couple times a week. She met lots of people in a wide cross section of professions and she had a ready-made subject to talk to them about (sports). She had opportunities for continued contact through the matches, so the relationships developed naturally over time. When she thought she wanted to go back to work, she mentioned she was thinking about it to her tennis friends. They were able to direct her to a few different options in her field, financial services. Their names helped get her through the door and into the interviews. Her résumé impressed potential employers, as did her tennis skills. She said bosses, especially in finance, like to see an interest in sports because it shows drive and dedication.

Our friend who became a golf diva to keep close to her husband tapped the friends she had made on the golf course when she wanted to go back to work. Our yoga girlfriends did the same thing. You may not think of the people you meet doing exercise as a network because you are comfortable talking to them, but guess what, you're networking.

ATHLETIC RESOURCES

- Luna tours offers beginning bicycle tours just for women, www.lunatours.com.
- American Alliance for Health, Physical Education, Recreation, and Dance gives a national overview on what's going on in female sports as well as links for Web sites in every state that list athletic opportunities for women, www.aahperd.org.
- American Running Association provides information about running groups and how to plan a race, www.americanrunning.org.
- Contact a local gym or community center to ask about local swim, tennis, soccer, and softball groups.

FREELANCE OR HOLIDAY WORK

KimMarie kept her contacts up with Godiva chocolates by doing contract work. KimMarie was a regional manager of Godiva stores when she quit. She was a mover in the company.

When she left to stay home with the kids, she made it clear that she wanted to work for Godiva during Christmas and Valentine's Day. What big executive thing was she doing? Stocking store shelves. That's right, she was unloading boxes of chocolates right along with her former employees.

A lot of women refuse to do work that's beneath the level they used to be at. This is a huge mistake. You have to be in front of people or on their minds to get offers and opportunities. Sitting alone in your house thinking about all the things you won't do isn't going to get you anything but more time alone.

You have to get out there.

Megan is a freelance writer and public relations person by trade. She has a philosophy: Say yes to everything, be fun, and follow up. Fortunately, her mother lives nearby and loves looking after the kids.

Whenever someone asks Megan for help with a job, she agrees, even if the job doesn't pay or isn't something she'd choose over a root canal. She says yes because often unpaid jobs turn into paid offers or referrals to other more lucrative opportunities. Same thing with doing a job you don't want to do. It can lead to other things.

Megan agreed to help a friend who needed someone to write a press release the next day for a university oceanography program. It wasn't the kind of writing Megan usually did but in keeping with her philosophy she said yes. She did it and her friend was so grateful she offered her more work, which snow-balled into a full-time job. The job includes an annual trip to Paris for a scientific conference.

WHERE DO THE KIDS GO?

There are several child-care options from which to choose.

Nannies

Not all nannies work full time. Some have part-time arrangements. Others will do a share arrangement if you can promise them full-time hours working for two or three other moms.

If you are fortunate enough to afford a nanny, a reputable

placement service can help match you with the right person to fit your needs. Even if the service you use is regarded as the best in town, be sure to ask lots of questions.

- Is the caregiver CPR certified?
- Does she have a good driving record should you need her to run errands or take the kids to sports practice?
- Does she have a criminal record? Doing time in the big house is probably not the kind of experience you want for working in your house.
- Be sure to personally check all her references. Keep in mind that a placement service will charge a fee, but it may be well worth the cost.

Years ago, Monica began her quest for a nanny by running an ad in the local newspaper. For the most part, very nice women who happened to be in the United States illegally responded to the ad. Since one of Monica's legal specialties is immigration law, she felt it would be particularly bad form to hire one of these women. Just as she began losing hope, she found the perfect candidate. The woman was in her early twenties, appeared to love children, and seemed very eager to work. During the interview, the woman spoke passionately about her church activities. Monica thought she'd finally found her nanny. As a last little formality, her husband did a background check on the woman. Turns out she was on probation for shoplifting, a fact she conveniently failed to mention in the interview. Needless to say, she didn't get the job and Monica went the placement service route.

Certainly, you don't need to hire a nanny or put your child in a day-care center. You quit work to avoid that scenario. But you can take advantage of other child-care options to meet your needs.

Mom's Day Out

Churches, synagogues, and community centers offer Mom's Day Out programs, which allow you to drop the kids off for a few hours on a set day and time each week. The programs are usually free, open to the community at large, and only run one day a week. Contact your community churches and synagogues to find out more information or ask friends with children to make recommendations.

Babysitting Co-op

You might also organize a babysitting co-op with other moms you know. Mothers take turns watching one another's children on designated days.

Family Connections

Your mother, mother-in-law, sister, or a close friend might also be willing to help care for your child once or twice a week while you take a class or do volunteer work. Your husband may also agree to pitch in and help some evenings or on weekends.

When Andrea moved from Delaware to Iowa, she needed to take a few evening courses to obtain her Iowa medical license. Her husband agreed to watch their one-year-old son, Sam, the evenings she was in class. She says when she approached her husband about making this commitment, he agreed because he knew that it would help her should she decide to return to work.

"My husband loves spending time one-on-one with Sam,"

Andrea told us. "He actually feels like he misses out on a lot of fun activities and milestones of Sam's because of his work schedule."

Nursery and Elementary School

It's true as your children grow older they don't need you every second of the day. When your child enrolls in nursery school you can plan to volunteer or do something out of the house while he's in school.

7
Part Time

It Ain't Perfect, but It's Doable

It's the nirvana we all are looking for. It's the holy grail. Every woman we talked to, every girlfriend of ours with children or thinking about them says what would be great is to have a part-time job they could work at while their children are in school and be back home in time to pick them up. And then, without fail, every one of them says there's nothing like that out there.

Not quite true.

What doesn't exist is the stress-free, prance in and flit out when you want job. Also imaginary is the job that will give you the same pay and advancement opportunities as those working full time, though this is starting to change in some industries. For instance, in some law firms it's now possible to work part time and still be on the partnership track.

Any job you have will involve stress and compromise. Some days working part time will be inconvenient. Occasionally you won't be able to pick your children up from school. Once in a while you'll feel like pulling the covers over your face and calling in sick. That's life. As Karen Hughes said to us, if your employer is willing to be flexible for you then you owe it to them to be flexible back.

Also, keep in mind that temporary jobs often turn into permanent positions. When employers like you, they'll find a way to hire you.

If you love what you do, part time is a way to continue doing it. Warts and all, it's a good way to keep your skills up, your foot in the door, and to make some money.

While things in the world of part-time employment have improved dramatically in the past few years, there still aren't as many part-time options out there as we'd like. Among full-time wage and salary employees, 18 percent would prefer to work part time; of those, 44 percent say their employers wouldn't let them, according to a 2002 study of 2,810 workers by the Families and Work Institute, a nonprofit group based in New York. The good news is that the employment experts we talked to say part-time options are increasing.

To retain more part-time workers, some law firms are using a test in the same vein as the quizzes in teen magazines to find out what they need to change to make jobs more enticing. The rate-your-job test measures how many hours part-time employees are actually working, what kind of assignments they get, how much they get promoted, and what their attrition rate is compared to full-time workers. Many of the law firms that used the test changed polices because of the results. Instead of having part-time employees work on a case-by-case basis with their choice of assignments from a selection of those that no one else wanted, the firms are now paying part-time workers more per hour and putting them on the partnership track like their full-time counterparts.

Accounting firms including PricewaterhouseCoopers assigned coordinators to track the progress of part-time workers. The coordinator ensures that the workers who are being paid part time aren't working full time and that they are getting their share of choice assignments. All this means it's getting easier, more acceptable, and more common to work part time or to cycle back to work after an absence—good news for us.

Aquent Marketing Staffing, Inc., a Chicago-based company, specializes in placing stay-at-home moms with marketing experience in full- or part-time temporary positions for project management, data analysis, research, and marketing communications across the country. They fill gaps due to surges in business and maternity, medical, or family leave. The company helps women brush up their résumés and brings them up to speed on industry and technology trends.

Willow CSN is a Florida call center company that allows its employees to work from home as they take rental car reservations, respond to complaints on consumer appliances, or answer the phone on behalf of the more than twenty companies that have contracted with Willow. There are many other call center companies, which now provide the option to work at home, including Alpine Access in Colorado, Working Solutions in Texas, and West Corp. in Nebraska. Companies like JetBlue, all of whose eight hundred reservation agents work from home, are jumping on this trend.

Women@Work Network, LLC, is a group that helps women update their résumés and interview skills. It also posts part-time, full-time, and interim job openings for members at www.womenatworknetwork.com.

Deloitte & Touche launched Personal Pursuits, a program that provides training, mentoring, career coaching, and networking events to moms who quit working for the company but hope to come back on a full-time or part-time basis.

RETURN TO THE SAME JOB

You've been home for a couple years or a few months and you're interested in doing something outside home—nothing all-encompassing. Is your old employer an option?

It depends on lots of factors.

Say you worked there for years, you have a specialized skill set, business is booming, and you have a great relationship with your former supervisor. Okay, if you have a combination of two of the above criteria you're doing pretty well. It also helps if another woman in the company has tried what you want to do and has been a raging success at it. On the other hand, it hurts your case if she was a flaming failure.

All that said, do your homework. Talk to the human resources person about the hypotheticals of part time. How hard would it be to be part time at your old company? Has anyone done it before?

Some signs that part time isn't a good deal at the company include: if fewer than 3 percent of employees work part time, if most of the part-timers are women, and if part-timers quit at higher rates than full-time workers. All these signs indicate that part-timers aren't taken seriously, valued, or treated well, because if they were more people would be working part time, men would jump on board, and employees would stay at the jobs if they were happy.

Put together a written proposal. Write everything down to help you organize your thoughts for your talk with your future employer. Consider giving a version of the proposal to the employer if it seems like it will help your case (see the box on p. 130). Also, read *Creating a Flexible Workplace* by Barney Olmstead and Suzanne Smith. This book offers excellent suggestions on now to approach scheduling and work load issues.

PROPOSAL TO WORK PART TIME

- Describe in detail how the work will be accomplished and how your responsibilities will be handled.
- Mention your future goals at the company. Would you like to go full time eventually?
- Be willing to negotiate on your schedule. If they prefer you to work three full days as opposed to four half days, if at all possible, agree. Make it clear in your proposal that you're flexible. You can always renegotiate terms later if they like your work.
- If you can work from home, describe how you think you can accomplish that, for example, do you have a home office? A dedicated phone line?
- Identify your own strengths. What skills do you have that few others do?
- Keep your emotions out of the negotiations.
- Propose a trial period of six to eight weeks.
- The most common complaint you'll get from employers is "If I let you do it, then everyone will want to." The answer is that most people can't afford to work part time and they're afraid of what will happen to their careers if they do. Plus, experts say a rush to part time doesn't happen when one person is allowed to do it.
- If you're close to former coworkers, you may want to feel them out about the part-time possibilities in the office before you talk to your boss.

Once you have your proposal in order, e-mail your former supervisor and ask her to lunch. You pay. At lunch, informally tell her what you want to do. Remember, this isn't an interview. You shouldn't expect her to give you a conclusive decision at the end of the lunch. It's enough that she'll think about your proposal. It's very likely that she'll have to bounce it off of other people in the office before she forms a definitive opinion. Relax and think of the lunch as a market research opportunity. You're testing your idea with an employer. You'll be able to figure out what's good in your approach and what needs work.

Give your former supervisor a couple weeks to call or e-mail you back. If you don't hear from her in that time period, don't assume that she hates the idea and you. As stay-at-home moms, our time horizon is dramatically different than it used to be. We want answers in a couple days, and we don't understand how it could take someone longer than that to figure out the future of our employment. Take a deep breath and think back to when you were at work. Remember how you'd have the best intentions to follow up on something, you'd make a mental note and a Post-it note and put it on your computer, and then days would go by before you even thought of it again. That's what your former supervisor is going through. Your request doesn't contribute to the bottom line or her boss's evaluation of her performance so it isn't on the top of her priority list.

After a couple weeks go by, e-mail her. Make sure the e-mail doesn't sound snippy, demanding, or whiny. Reread it several times, have your husband read it, and then sit on it a day before you send it. Wait another week for a response. If you don't get one, call her and ask what she thinks about your proposal.

Don't feel discouraged. J.C. has a friend who spent a year discussing a part-time position with her former boss. They went to lunch several times and discussed the myriad of possibilities. She could work half days every day; she could come in two full days and one half; she could telecommute for a portion of it. They went round and round. Her boss needed to think about it; she had to talk to her higher up. J.C.'s friend didn't end up working there. It was frustrating, especially since she'd been telling people for months that she'd be going back to work any day. The discussions did teach her what to ask for and to be patient.

A few months after negotiations with her old employer fell apart, she found another part-time possibility through a friend. This time negotiations only took a couple weeks. A year later and she's still there.

Secretary of Education Margaret Spellings worked part time on two occasions when her daughters were young—once for a few months, and then for a year.

She said she pitched her bosses about taking over projects that were short-term and therefore didn't provide a lot of stability. She knew that for her coworkers who were primary breadwinners, the projects weren't desirable because when they were done in six months or a year, there was no guarantee there'd be another opportunity. That'd leave the question of where the mortgage payment was coming from up in the air.

"I chose flexibility over stability," Margaret said.

She also found ways to shave off portions of work into discrete projects that could be done on her time schedule and at home.

"You have to make the case that you have a project you can do and that needs to be done," she said.

Amy, an analyst for a Fortune 500 company, can vouch for the frustrations of trying to negotiate part time with your old employer. In 1991, she proposed a part-time arrangement after the birth of her second child. The company agreed. The only hitch was that the office she worked in never had a part-time employee at her level before.

"Once they agreed, they couldn't figure out what do to with me," she said.

Things got off to a rocky start the first day. After an hour of condescending instruction on how to fill out new employee forms because she was now classified as a temporary worker, she picked up her things and headed to work.

"I told them that I would go ahead and fill out the forms myself and if I did anything wrong they could just let me know," she said.

In the first few weeks her supervisor kept assigning her work, taking it away, and shifting her from one project to another.

"He was trying to figure out how much I could accomplish in twenty hours. I felt like I was playing musical assignments," Amy said.

A few months into it things were finally going well, or so she thought. Her subordinates weren't quite as happy. Amy's workers could only contact her when she was in the office, not on a daily basis like other bosses. Some of them felt that her part-time status hurt their own chances for advancement. It was a tough issue to smooth out with them. She could reassure them their advancement wasn't being hindered, but only time could prove her right.

A year later, Amy left the company's employee payroll and became an independent management consultant for the firm. The company had changed its policy on part-time work and insisted Amy either come back full time or quit. She suggested they keep her on as a consultant and since she was no longer an employee they wouldn't have to pay her benefits. She was able to make this pitch because her husband already had health insurance to cover the family. She did lose other benefits the company offered, and because she was self-employed she had to file quarterly tax returns at a higher rate. She also recognized that by becoming a consultant, she lost job security. Despite the company's initial agreement to take her on to do consulting work, there was always the possibility that it would be easier for them to find her services no longer needed than it would be if she was a paid member of the staff.

Nevertheless, she decided to take the risk and, to her amazement, she earned more money in that role than she had working part time.

"And I had more flexibility and fewer hassles," she said.

When You're Ready to Take the Job

You have a good feeling and you're ready to take the job. The final discussion you need to have with your prospective employer is one that outlines exactly when you work, how much you work, and what happens when you go over those hours. Be very specific about what you're asking for. Is it important for you to take your children to school? Schedule your work hours to start after you drop them off. Do you want to go on field trips with your child? Let your employer know.

The career counselors we've talked to say it's important to have set hours you're in the office that everyone knows about so they can see you when they need to. It's also better, if you can do it, to be in the office every day because you pick up on little things that people wouldn't put in an e-mail or call you about but that can affect how well you do your job.

Edith arranged to work from 1:00 to 6:00 P.M., five days a week. She's a computer networker and people start calling the office a lot in the afternoon, which is why she thought it was important to be there after lunch. A couple of days a week she also made a point to come in at noon and have lunch with her coworkers so she could keep abreast of workplace dynamics.

Hillary decided to work in the mornings because that's when

the meetings for the human resources department were held. When she started part time she had tried to work two and a half days a week but her coworkers could never keep straight when she was supposed to be in the office and when she was out. After two months, she changed to showing up every morning because she thought the daily face time with her coworkers would alleviate their confusion. It did. At the morning meetings, she was able to clear up any issues that had developed the previous afternoon.

Worming Your Way Back In

If your former employer didn't warm to the idea of part time, it's time to look elsewhere. This makes your search more challenging. Other companies don't know you. They have no idea what kind of worker you are. They don't have any loyalty to you personally. You have to present a compelling case as to why you are worth taking a risk on.

Think hard about what you have to offer.

Danielle is a nurse. For some years now there has been a nursing shortage in this country. Many hospitals are actively recruiting mothers with nursing degrees out of their homes and into the workforce. Danielle had been at home for five years when she decided to go back to work. She didn't have to look too hard. Hospitals were bending over backward to get her to pick up shifts. She was able to craft a schedule around her children. She started working two nights a month at a hospital to ease her family into the change in lifestyle—basically she thought her husband could only handle cooking a couple of nights. She did that for four months. When the hospital had an opening, she picked up more shifts. She ended up working thirty hours a week, two nights and the rest of the time when her children were in school.

Emily used to work for a bank. She was the vice president of marketing and she had her securities and insurance licenses. By the time she wanted to go back to work her licenses had expired and her former employer was happy with her replacement, so she couldn't slip back into her old job or anything like it. Through a friend, she met a life insurance agent who mentioned his company had recently started offering financial planning and investment advice as part of its services. The planners were paid solely on commissions. She decided this would be a perfect way to get back into work. She could use the knowledge she had from getting her licenses but she didn't need them to be current. Since she was working on commission, she could set her own hours and not feel guilty about taking time off because she wasn't an expense to the company, she wasn't getting a salary or any benefits like health insurance.

She worked on commission for two years and built a loyal client base. Her employer was happy. Other companies heard about her performance and started talking to her about working for them. Her track record was her best calling card. If she didn't perform, she didn't get paid.

"That I was able to make a good income spoke volumes to other companies about how good I was at my job," she says.

Her old employer even offered her old position to her after her replacement moved to Boston. She took it. At first, she worked thirty hours a week. When her children went to school, she ramped up to forty hours.

We know two—count them, two—women who secured part-time positions at law firms where they had not previously worked. They are both named Debbie.

The first Debbie moved from New York to Philadelphia after the birth of her second child and snagged a part-time position.

She said she applied to all the firms she was interested in working for, waited until they contacted her, and then told them she wanted to work part time. Out of the five firms she contacted, three said they were okay with her working reduced hours.

"I knew Philly was a family-friendly city and that law firms there value New York lawyers," she said.

In addition to working part time, she also started Flex-Time Lawyers, which is a group that supports lawyers who work a reduced schedule and seek work/life balance. The group meets monthly. Debbie established two chapters in New York and Philadelphia. She also consults with law firms that want to obtain better retention rates for women.

"I see a lot of firms wanting to change their ways. They're losing women in droves, which is adding to their costs. It takes a lot of time and money to train a lawyer," she said.

Our second Debbie, a mother of three, applied for and got a part-time position at a small law firm in 1985—the stone ages as far as part time is concerned. She worked part time for eight years under a boss she liked. She got good assignments by picking up the slack for other lawyers. When she saw that her coworkers were overwhelmed, she offered to take pieces of the projects they were working on. Her boss noticed.

"He came up to me and said, 'You're not supposed to be doing that. Can you handle it?' I said, 'I'm eighty percent done. I'll finish it by the end of the week,'" she said. He was impressed and handed her bigger and more challenging assignments.

The firm even fought for her when they were in negotiations to merge with another law office. Twelve years ago, she went full time. After a year and a half of full-time work, they offered her a partnership.

FINDING A PART-TIME JOB

- Many career counselors recommend going on interviews for full-time jobs as well as part time because if a company likes you, they'll adapt their hours to get you.
- Think of part time, three-quarters time, and flex-time as part of the job negotiations like when you try to bargain for extra vacation time. When you start to think of it as another negotiation point it becomes easier to ask for and you also can craft an argument for it including some of the things you may give up, for example, vacation time.
- Part time and flex-time are becoming much more prevalent. Don't feel self-conscious about pursuing these alternatives. If a prospective employer gives you a hard time, know there are many more out there that are much more accepting.
- The best way to find a new part-time job is to network with your old coworkers, other mothers, your husband's coworkers and friends.
- You can also check out Web sites like www.monster.com, which list job openings around the country.
- If you are a member of a professional association, that would also be a good place to check.

I GET PAID PART-TIME BUT I WORK FULL-TIME

A lot of times we get into situations that are supposed to be part time but turn out to be part-time wages for full-time work. We call it sanctioned slave labor.

WORK SUPPORT GROUPS

- Flex-time lawyers, www.flextimelawyers.com
- Part-time moms, www.mom-in-the-middle.com
- National Association of Part-Time and Temporary Employees, www.members.tripod.com/~NAPTE/
- Association of Part-Time Librarians, www.canisius.edu/huberman/aptl.html

When one friend, Nicole, tried to leave work at 3:00 P.M., which was the agreed-upon time, her manager pulled her into her office. The manager, also a mother, explained to her that it would be in her best interest if she could show her commitment to work and stay until at least 5:00 P.M. She told Nicole that even when her own children were sick, she didn't take days off. When Nicole pointed out to her that she was only being paid part time, the manager smiled and told her good night.

After that discussion, Nicole noticed a significant drop in the quality and importance of the work she was given. Her manager became dismissive of her and joked about her leaving at three. Nicole overheard her calling it her "nap time." She noticed that the manager started scheduling meetings at 4:00 P.M., long after Nicole was supposed to be gone.

Needless to say, Nicole didn't last at the job long.

Another friend, Samantha, was penalized for doing only her part-time hours. As a practice manager at a doctor's office, Samantha was in charge of completing billings, updating patient records, and coordinating schedules. The doctors in the group agreed to allow her to work part time as long as she continued to

GUIDELINES FOR PART-TIME EMPLOYEES

- Before taking the job, ask to speak with other part-time employees and moms who already work there. Go out to lunch if you can because you get them out of the office where others can't listen to what they're saying. Ask them how the company's policies really work. What do they say when you want to leave at 3:00 P.M.?
- Once you decide to take the job, be as explicit as you can with your employer about the parameters of the part-time arrangement, particularly with respect to the hours you'll be working and what happens when you go over those hours. If you can, get the agreement in writing.
- While working there, have set hours so coworkers know when and where they can reach you.
- Fully live up to your commitment. Work the hours you agreed to work.
- If the employer makes demands on you that result in you exceeding the agreed-upon hours, remind the employer about

do the billings and patient records. They thought they could handle scheduling.

Samantha worked in the office afternoons from 1:00 to 5:00 P.M. She was able to finish all the agreed-upon paperwork during her allotted hours. She worked in this arrangement for a year and thought it was going great. She was able to spend mornings with her son. After lunch she dropped him off at her mother-in-law's house.

The doctors weren't happy. Over the previous year they had

the terms of the agreement. Don't be confrontational. Instead, simply say, "Remember we agreed I would work three days a week." By putting it in terms of "we" she'll be reminded that she agreed to this arrangement too.

- On the occasions when you do agree to make an exception to your arrangement, remind your boss in a nice way that you're making an exception. Otherwise, he may begin to automatically assume that you'll always be available to work additional hours when he needs you.
- Respect your full-time coworkers as such. While you needn't behave like a second-class citizen on the job, you can't expect to run the place either.
- Always remember that your supervisor's role is to utilize each member of his staff in order to accomplish the task assigned to him by the company. When he doesn't seem to care that your child is sick or is performing in a school play you want to see, he's not necessarily being a heartless jerk. He may simply be concerned about how he's going to get the job done.

fumbled with the schedule several times. They fought over who was going to deal with equipment repairs. They fired Samantha and they told her they were looking for a full-time practice manager. When she suggested that instead of letting her go they hire another part-time person, they said it was too much hassle.

"I think they had built up so much resentment for me over the past year because they hated doing scheduling and all the other stuff I used to do that they wanted me out of there. They weren't open to any kind of adaptations," Samantha said.

Secretary of Education Margaret Spellings, speaking as a former part-timer, says don't give yourself short shrift. When you work part time be realistic about what you can accomplish in the time you're being paid for. If you work more than that amount, tell your employer and ask to be compensated.

If your boss doesn't understand that may be a signal to start looking for another job. Spellings said that President George W. Bush has always been flexible with her about work hours even when she had to leave early every other Friday for months to travel back to Texas for her daughters. That's why she's still working for him eleven years later.

WORKING FROM HOME

There are different considerations if you're working from home. Karen Hughes said the one thing she regrets about working at home was that she didn't physically separate her work area from her home. A war could be going on in her kitchen and she wouldn't know it. She could concentrate in any situation. As a result, she didn't have a dedicated office and worked while her family was around her. Work and family blended almost seamlessly. When her son was a toddler, she could keep one eye on him while she was on a conference call. A lot of us wish we could multitask like that but Karen says it has its downside.

"I was too distracted when my son was little. I wish I spent more time focused on him," she says.

Our friend Terry has an office in her house that is strictly for work. When she goes in there and shuts the door, her children know not to disturb her. Her husband understands that he should only knock on the door in an emergency. She has set office hours from 9:00 A.M. to 2:00 P.M. A nanny is in the house while Terry is working and her children have adjusted to her schedule. The only time there's an issue is if her son tries to bounce a tennis ball in the house. Terry can hear it in her office downstairs.

Another woman only works if her children are asleep, at school, or at their grandparents. It's an erratic schedule. One day she'll have five hours of uninterrupted time; the next day she might only have two. Despite the unpredictability, she says she manages to get in about twenty-five hours a week.

"When I'm home and my kids are up I want to focus on them. They're the reason why I'm working from home," she says.

Be honest with yourself about what type of person you are— structured or fluid. If you're structured, make sure you have a dedicated workspace with everything you need in it. Like a girl-

---

FLUID WAYS OF WORKING

- Identify a room or space in your house, for example, a spare bedroom or desk in the living room, that you can claim as your own. Only use this space for work.
- Explain to your family why this is your space and why it's important that they respect it.
- Buy office supplies and use them strictly in that place.
- Consider installing a dedicated or second phone line because then you're the only one answering the phone and you'll feel more like you're in an office.
- Establish office hours, meaning tell your family when you're working and explain to them that they can't talk to you when you're in the office unless it's an emergency.

friend of ours said, "When you have the right tools, work is easy." Be sure you have a child-care situation that will allow you uninterrupted time. Don't think you'll figure it out as you go along, you'll only end up frustrated.

I DON'T GET TENURE FOR PART-TIME WORK, WHY BOTHER?

We went to coffee with one woman who promised us she was going to tell us what it's like to work part time. Adrian was going to unload the nasty awful truth about cruel employers, unsympathetic coworkers, and clueless husbands. She promised we'd be depressed about our options after we left. She told us that there are no happy endings.

We prepared ourselves. This is what we suspected. We wondered if underlying all those promises about women being able to take time off work, stay home with their kids, and then go back to work was a reality a whole lot less rosy. Finally there was a woman ready to admit that it wasn't possible to have half of it all.

We waited. She was late. Ten minutes, a half hour went by. We looked up and were surprised to see a jittery, agitated woman with two-inch roots walk in. Was this our friend?

Adrian sat down. She had rings under her eyes. Her face had aged five years in six months. She had lost weight and her skin had a grayish undertone. She looked intently at both of us and it seemed like she was near tears. Then she spoke. Her voice was tinged with the bitterness we detected on the phone.

She regaled us with her attempt to go part time at the university where she had tenure. She said the university agreed to it, but it was difficult. Her class schedule was not just bad, it was intentionally impossible. Her other duties, like office hours, overlapped on time she had mapped out to spend with her children. The hourlong commute was intolerable to make every day if she was only going to be there two hours at a time.

"They were horrible. They won't change my schedule. They won't let me cut my office hours. They ruined my career," she said vehemently.

She quit because the situation was impossible. As she ran her fingers repeatedly through her hair and tapped her feet, she repeated that her academic career was over. We tried to cheer her up. We told her she was exaggerating. She cut us off.

"I can't work there again. I won't do part time somewhere else because I'll never get tenure, and I'm not doing that, so my academic career is over," Adrian said as her eyes became watery.

She announced that she started a catering business with her husband. She radiated anger and resentment.

Does she even like cooking?

"I like running a business with my husband. The business was his idea," she said. Her husband is a professionally trained chef.

She said she misses the academic work, her students, and dressing up to go to work. Now she constantly has dough under her nails and the most intellectual stimulation she gets from her job is doing the books.

"This is my life," she said as she laid her palms flat on the table and bowed her forehead in between them. You know what we took away from all this—our friend is one bitter woman.

Of course, there were problems with her situation. Her commute was long. But hadn't it been long when she worked full time? Her class schedule was insane. But couldn't she adjust it the next semester? What was wrong with working part time somewhere else without tenure?

Adrian, like so many of us, feels she has reached a point in her career and life where things shouldn't be so difficult. She thinks she should have seniority at this stage in her life. Unfortunately she doesn't.

Don't get us wrong. We're all for leaving a job where the boss treats you badly and your coworkers are venomous, but we aren't for giving up because things get hard. A lot of times when you go part time there's a transition period in which you're back to paying your dues. You put up with the crappy schedule and assignments for a few months; you show that you have a good attitude. Then things improve. If they don't, you talk to your boss again. If things still don't improve, quit.

We have to tell you, as your friend, don't be a princess. Don't give up your career because everything isn't perfect. Remodel it.

IMPROVING PART TIME

- If people complain that they never know when you're there, adjust your work schedule so you're in the office every morning or every afternoon.
- Find two mentors. Seek out an administrative assistant who's been there awhile and who can show you the ropes and give you personality breakdowns on everyone. Find a peer who can do the same thing from a different vantage point.
- Make sure you don't take your work home with you. Up until now you've either worked full time or not at all. Don't fall into the trap of feeling you're back at work, which means full time.
- In the first couple months, check in with your boss once a week and see what needs to be changed and what's working.
- If it's not working after six months, don't be afraid to quit.

THE SERIAL SUCCESSFUL PART-TIMER

Elena is a very focused woman. She's one of those people who actually writes down her New Year's resolutions on January 1 and then does them. She decided she wanted to have a baby two years before she did it. She finished her PhD and opted to live close to where she studied because she had a large pool of contacts she could tap into and her husband had good job options in the area.

She knew she wanted a part-time job and put out feelers to her contacts. One put her in touch with Johns Hopkins University and she was hired for a temporary, six-month-long job. She took it. It didn't have job security, definitely not tenure, but she made some money while she looked for the next job and made good contacts. She impressed her bosses so much that when her six-month position ended, they found another position for her.

This is an important point to make about temporary jobs. Oftentimes temporary jobs turn into permanent positions. If the employer likes you, she'll usually find a way to keep you and if she can't, she'll refer you to others or try to hire you later. A temporary job is definitely worth the time.

Getting back to Elena, she accepted the job at Johns Hopkins and worked there part time for another year. But she was getting restless. She wanted to find something a little closer to home and more in her field of study, which is teaching people how to be science educators.

She started going on interviews for full-time jobs. She thought if she got herself in front of people in organizations she wanted to work for, they'd know who she was and when a part-time job came open they'd think of her. The strategy worked twice.

Another thing we want to emphasize: Apply for everything in

your field. Full time or part time, it doesn't matter. Get in front of people. When a manager likes you, he'll try to hire you. Even if you're not right for the opening at hand, he'll mentally file away your name and call you when another job becomes available. It also helps if you e-mail occasionally after you interview.

Elena applied for a job developing educational software even though it was advertised as a full-time position. The firm liked her so much they were willing to reduce the hours and work around her schedule. She had been working at the job two years when a contact she made applying for jobs a couple years before called her and offered her a part-time teaching position at a nearby university.

Don't be afraid to quit. Elena's employers knew what she was looking for and they knew that the positions they offered her weren't ideal. The commutes were more than an hour and the work wasn't exactly in her field. When she quit she gave each employer a month's notice and offered to help anytime after that.

She accepted the teaching position, of course. She now works three days a week, ten minutes from her home. She drops her son off at day care on the campus, checks in with him at lunch, and walks the quarter of a mile to the day care from her office to pick him up.

Sounds idyllic, and to her it is. But she doesn't have tenure. She doesn't make the biggest salary. If she was our friend Adrian she'd be miserable. This proves to us what our grandmothers always told us and we never believed: your attitude as much as the circumstance is what makes you happy.

IS MY CAREER OVER BECAUSE
I WORK PART-TIME?

Anita McBride is Laura Bush's chief of staff. It's a high-profile, sensitive position. Many would camp out in front of the White House for days just to have a chance at an interview. What did Anita do to land the title? Well, she worked part time for eight years, volunteered free of charge for several months, and took a year off work completely.

To all of us who toss and turn in our beds, staying up half the night wondering if we're doing the right thing, if our careers are over because we scaled back, the answer is no. You can go back to work. You can wind up in your most desired dream job. Anita McBride is a case in point.

Anita didn't chart her career. She isn't one of those women who has a five-year plan or a ten-year job goal.

Instead, she just always wanted to work. She wanted to keep her finger in the professional pool. Keeping up her contacts and remaining flexible is what helped put her in the position she's in today.

When her husband needed to relocate to Philadelphia from Washington, D.C., she got a part-time job at SmithKline Beacham, a pharmaceutical company. She managed projects in their philanthropy division, including a summer science program for inner-city kids at local libraries.

They moved back to D.C. three years later. Shortly after the move, Anita gave birth to the first of her two children. She decided she wanted to be at home with her baby and took a part-time job for an executive search firm that allowed her to work from her house two days a week. She stayed with them for five years.

She had gained personnel experience in the Reagan and first Bush administrations, rising to the position of director of White House Personnel.

"I was fortunate to land in personnel. It's ideal work to stay connected. Everyone who comes into a business or leaves it talks to you. It's like you're a den mother," Anita said.

When George W. Bush was elected, Anita had no plans to join the administration, but a friend called and asked if she would come help out the transition team on a volunteer basis a couple of mornings a week. Two mornings morphed into three days and that evolved into all week. After a few months of volunteering Anita was offered a paid position.

She began at the White House and then moved to the State Department, handling presidential placements. Just two weeks into the job, the White House called asking her to take the position of special assistant to the president for White House Management. She would be responsible for all aspects of running the White House from telephones and office assignments to infrastructure matters and managing the White House budget. She accepted the position despite her reservations as mother of two young children.

"It was the toughest job I've ever done," she said. "I was here every night until one or two o'clock in the morning. My youngest child was just seven months old at that point. Finally, I realized it was too much. I went to the chief of staff and told him that although I loved the Bushes, I just couldn't keep doing this."

She returned to the State Department and was there eighteen months when her husband accepted a yearlong job in Germany for DaimlerChrysler. Anita told her bosses at the State Department that she'd be back in a year and she'd love to return to work there. The department worked out an arrangement where she could keep her security clearances current.

When she came back, she was given a position in the State Department for two days a week recruiting Americans to work in United Nations posts. She was content. Working part time satisfied her desire to keep working and suited her family. She wasn't looking for anything else.

Driving to pick up her kids one day, Anita's cell phone rang. Mrs. Bush's office wanted to know if Anita was interested in being considered for the position as her chief of staff after the 2004 election.

Anita was honored but hesitant. Her husband traveled frequently. She knew if she was offered the position she'd be working a lot and if her husband was traveling a lot there wouldn't be a steady parental presence at home.

She went ahead and interviewed with Mrs. Bush, who offered her the job a few weeks later. At the same time, her husband accepted a new job that kept him off the road. They both started in their new positions on the same day.

Her advice?

Don't be afraid to volunteer, always keep doing something for yourself, like a part-time job, and when you do work make sure you have good help because employers and coworkers can lose patience quickly with home emergencies.

8
Going Back

*The When and How of
Returning to Work Full Time*

This is the most commonly asked and philosophically debated question among our girlfriends since "Friendship or sexual attraction, which is more important in a prospective husband?"

Is it worth it to go back to work?

A lot of times the salary you start at when you go back will barely cover the child-care costs you'll incur. Your husband may whine and moan and tell you to stay home because he doesn't want to deal with the extra hassle of child care, more tax forms, and more responsibility. Funny, since he probably complained when you quit. Your children may beg you to stay home and promise that if you go back to work it will be the end of the world as they know it and they can't make you any guarantees about how they'll turn out as a result. They'll dangle the specter of juvenile delinquency in front of you.

All these factors cause a lot of our friends to sigh with resignation at the afterschool pick up spot and say they think it's best for the family if they don't go back.

But is that really what's best?

Our children will never want us to go back to work. They will always have issues when we do. Our husbands will have problems too. However much they grumble about us staying at home, they have it easier logistically and child-wise when we do stay home. Men do not like things that disrupt their lives. That's why they stay loyal to losing sports teams, shaving creams, and brands of underwear for decades. When you leave and enter the workforce you're inflicting a lot of change on them.

One friend's wife has stayed at home with their three children for eight years. She talks about going back to work but her husband, our friend, constantly pooh-poohs the idea because it would be a hassle. She's a teacher. At the height of her career, she didn't make more than $40,000. He makes $250,000.

"We don't need the money. If she went back, taking the kids everywhere they need to go would be a nightmare. It's not worth it," he said.

That's the crux of the issue. A lot of times it's not worth it for him if you go back to work, but it is worth it for you. When you return to work you revive your contacts and add new ones to your address book. You test yourself intellectually. You form new neural pathways.

Is it worth it?

Absolutely. If you want to go back, don't let family fears stop you. They'll readjust after a few months. Six months go by and it will be like you always worked.

MAKING THE DECISION TO RETURN TO WORK

For some women, the decision to stay home with the kids is a permanent one. In addition to their last paycheck, their employer should hand them a gold watch as they walk out the door. This is their retirement. They're never going back, and they know it.

Most women don't fit this category. They know that someday they'll come back. The question is not if but when.

Typically, these women struggle with when to return to work almost as much as the initial quandary over whether to leave in the first place. For each woman, the factors driving her decision to return to work are quite personal.

Give yourself time to evaluate your reasons and make sure you're prepared. One employer said he sees a lot of women come back to work when they're not ready to work. Their hearts aren't

SOME REASONS WOMEN RETURN TO WORK

- Boredom—the kids are either in school all day or grown and out of the house completely
- Money—your husband loses his job or you find it impossible to survive on one income
- Circumstances—you're divorced or a widow
- Opportunity—a once in a lifetime job opportunity arises
- Reality—you want to stay in your profession and you realize if you don't return to work soon your degree and job experience will be obsolete

in it; their heads are somewhere else. They aren't as competitive as they used to be.

Anna and her husband decided that her staying home with their three daughters was important.

"It was actually his idea," she says. "He had a single mom who worked all the time and was never able to be home with him and his brothers. He felt strongly that one parent needed to be home with the kids."

Then he lost his job. But that didn't send Anna immediately back into the workplace. Her husband found some contract work. Anna offered to return to work, but he insisted that things would be fine. Since Anna paid the bills, she knew that in fact things weren't fine at all and kept getting worse. Finally, when their savings dried up and making the mortgage payment became a strain, Anna went back to work.

"I knew we were headed into bankruptcy, and I didn't want to go there," she says. "Maybe someday I'll go back to being a stay-at-home mom again, but I'll definitely have to look long and hard at everything before I do it again."

SO WHAT DOES SHE DO ALL DAY?

Women usually start contemplating going back to work when their children are all in elementary school full time. It's about that time that they begin having a gnawing feeling that everyone is whispering behind their backs, "When is she going to go back to work?" or "So what keeps her busy from 9:00 A.M. to 3:00 P.M. every day?"

If you feel like you want to dip back into professional waters, start by discussing the possibility with your husband. Just as he had a critical vote in your decision to leave work, his opinion is extremely vital in whether or not you go back. With reservations, he'll probably support your returning to work. The additional income will take some of the strain off of him.

Only one factor is likely to stand in the way of him joining the team 100 percent and that is his willingness to make some pretty dramatic changes himself. He's accustomed to you always being there. He counts on dinner being ready when he arrives home from work. He knows he can ask you to run his car over for service in the middle of the day or pick up the laundry the moment it's ready. He never worries that the children aren't getting their homework done, receiving all their vaccinations on schedule, or eating their vegetables.

If you return to work, that all will change and he will have to agree to it. He'll have to help out at home. If not, you might as well prepare yourself for your nervous breakdown.

The number one mistake a woman makes in deciding to return to work is failing to work out the details of the new family situation with her spouse in advance. Instead, she tries to do everything herself. That arrangement works for a while. Then one day she's awakened by the scent of scores of flowers wafting from the windowsill of the hospital room where she's recovering from surgery to repair her bleeding ulcer.

Be reasonable and realistic. If you will only be working part time, you realistically can't expect your husband to agree to go fifty-fifty on everything. By the same token, if you will be working eight-hour days but only making a third of the salary your husband makes, don't immediately accept the argument that you should take on all the responsibility at home because his job brings home more money to the family.

ISSUES TO DISCUSS WITH YOUR HUSBAND

- Who will take care of the children's needs, like staying home with them when they're sick? Will you both equally share this responsibility or will it solely rest on your shoulders?
- What if your new job requires you to travel? Is your husband willing to be totally responsible for the needs of the household while you're away?
- What if both of you have jobs that require travel and there will be occasions when you're both out of town? What arrangements will you make for the children then?
- Who will cook the meals, wash the dishes, clean the clothes, vacuum the carpet, scrub the toilets, and perform all the other necessary tasks that keep the family fed, well dressed, and living without the constant fear that the Health Department might show up one day and declare the home unsafe for human habitation?
- Will you or your husband be responsible for all the duties associated with home maintenance? For instance, if you awake one day and discover that your dishwasher is leaking and that your hardwood kitchen floor is flooded, which one of you is going to wait to let the maintenance man in the house?
- Who will pay the bills each month?

CHILD CARE

The last factor in your decision is perhaps the most difficult—child care. You stayed home because you recognized the importance of being home with your child. A few years away from work and at home with the kids probably means that your needs and expectations for child care have changed.

If your child isn't school age, you will need full-time child care.

To hire a nanny or not? Unfortunately, one of the biggest factors in child care decisions is cost. Most women would love to hire a nanny so that their kids could have one-on-one attention in their own homes, but they discover it's way too expensive. A few years ago, Monica was shocked to learn that some nannies in her area earn $40,000 per year. That's fine for Bill and Melinda Gates perhaps, but even two highly paid working professionals struggle to scratch together that kind of money for child care. At the other end of the financial spectrum are day-care centers, which provide cost-effective but less personalized care. One mother described day care as detention for the pre-k set. In all fairness, we know of some pretty fabulous day cares that even teach the kids sign language and Spanish.

Given the combination of motherly guilt mixed with financial constraints, choosing child care is probably the most difficult task on your return-to-work checklist. Don't stress too much. As long as you research the place you choose and find it's safe, your child will prosper.

The Phylum of Child Care

- Nannies come in all varieties. There are full-time nannies who come to your house each day for a set number of hours, and there are part-time nannies who only come for part of each day. Unlike other child-care arrangements, a nanny provides one-on-one care for your children. One source for hiring a nanny is a placement service, but keep in mind that they charge a fee for checking references and doing a background check.

- An au pair is similar to a nanny except that she is typically a student from another country. She is working on a visa, which allows her to stay in the United States for a period of up to one year. Because she is essentially an exchange student, she lives with your family. Her work is restricted to child care. Don't ask her to clean the bathtub. Other restrictions on her employment are spelled out on the U.S. Department of State Web site (www.state.gov).

- Day-care centers are another option. Ask for the names of a few families who you can call to ask about the quality of the care there. Check with the state to see if the center has had any regulatory violations and, if so, what they were.

- Some mothers make their job taking care of children in their home. Talk to other parents who keep their children there. Make sure the home is childproofed and that the caregiver isn't trying to bring in a few extra dollars by taking in more children than she can handle.

If your children are in school, your child-care challenges will be different. Everything's fine from 9:00 A.M. to 3:00 P.M., but what do you do when the last school bell rings? Will they become latchkey kids, biding their time alone until you or your husband return from work? Or will you hire a part-time nanny or babysitter to take care of things in those hours until you return home? In our interviews with moms, we found many wanted to be home for their children or have some other responsible person around when they arrive home. The mothers felt a sense of panic worrying about what their kids might be up to.

Holidays and summer breaks are especially challenging. You might try hiring a college or responsible high school student to help out since he or she generally will be on a similar academic schedule as your child and may be looking for work during his or her breaks. In the summer, some parents send their children to summer camp. Some are day camps while other camps keep the kids overnight. Since most camps don't run all summer, some parents send their kids to more than one camp, although this can get expensive.

Whatever you choose, you need to be completely comfortable with your overall arrangement. Your effectiveness on the job will in large measure be determined by your confidence that all is well at home.

PREPARING THE KIDS

When you go back to work no one may take it harder than your children, depending on how you handle the situation and prepare them. They may take it as a personal affront that you've decided to work over spending time with them. Given that, once you've decided you are indeed returning to work, how do you present the news to them? Moreover, how do you get them ready for this change in their lives?

The most important factor in successfully handling the situation is your own attitude. Are you absolutely certain you want to go back to work? Have you made that decision and do you intend to stick with it?

"You have to be okay with the fact you're going back to work or the kids will pick up on your indecisiveness and negative feelings associated with returning to work," says Dr. Hellen Streicher, a child psychologist.

"Don't be in an emotional place where you find yourself confiding in your children, 'I hate to go back to work' or 'I'm nervous about this,' or convey this message to them with nonverbal communication, because most children are very sensitive and tuned in to their parents and will pick up on this. When they do, they might react to your negative feelings and attitude by becoming regressive, emotional, or by starting to act out," she says.

Dr. Streicher notes that "a typical secondary reaction might be for your stress level or feelings of guilt about leaving your children to return to work to increase even more, which could further exacerbate your child's stress level. It can become a vicious cycle unless you know to watch for this pattern and nip it in the bud if you become aware that these dynamics are occurring."

A few mothers have no qualms whatsoever about returning to work, but these women are the exception rather than the rule. If you've cared enough to leave a job or career you enjoyed in the first place to stay home with your kids, it's unlikely that you will take the decision to return to work lightly.

So how do you deal with any mixed feelings you might be experiencing? Dr. Streicher suggests simply reframing your thinking. Rather than viewing the event as a catastrophe and staying focused on the negative ("My child will be so upset with me and be emotionally scarred for life"), instead think about the positive ("Child care can provide my child with more learning opportunities to make new friends and to develop better social skills, self-esteem, and independence. Why would I want to stand in the way?"). Also, recognize that most research has failed to show any devastating negative effects on children's overall adjustment when both parents are working outside the home in some capacity. Remember that during World War II many women had to take jobs while their husbands served the country in the military, and their children (our parents) turned out okay.

Some mothers begin the conversation with their kids about their decision not as an announcement but as a question. "What do you think about mommy going back to work?" they'll ask. This is probably not the best tack: We don't have to tell you what the answer will be nine times out of ten.

"It is neither appropriate nor healthy for parent–child dynamics to give a child (especially younger children) decision-making power about whether or not a parent should return to work outside the home," says Dr. Streicher. "This is an adult matter and it is too stressful and anxiety provoking for a child to participate in this process. For example, what if a child said that she wanted the mother to return to work and things go wrong for Mom? What if she ends up feeling stressed out by her job, doesn't get along with her boss, spends more time than she anticipated commuting, or simply hates her job? The result could be that your child may feel responsible for this bad outcome, over which she didn't actually have any control. This can lead to unhealthy self-doubt and unnecessary guilt on the child's part. On the other hand, the child's reply could be 'No, I don't want you to go back to work.' Are you then going to allow your child to dictate your decision and actually not return to work? Probably not. It would be like asking your child if he wanted vanilla or chocolate ice cream, and then giving him the opposite of what was requested. It is unfair to give your child an illusion of control then ignore his or her wishes, which sets up your child for tremendous disappointment. Finally, if you have more than one child, involving them in this type of decision-making process can be further complicated if they each have different decisions. How would you handle 'choosing' one child's decision over the other child's?"

Instead of involving your child in the decision-making process (or giving the illusion that he or she is involved), Dr. Streicher suggests making a short, simple announcement that you are going back to work and framing it in a positive manner. Expound on the positives, like the added spending money the family will have, rather than sharing any negative feelings or reservations you might have. Saying "If your daddy wasn't such a big spender, I wouldn't have to go back to work" is probably a nonstarter.

Let your children ask questions, because many of their reservations are simply a result of their fear of the unknown: Where will they be while you're at work? Who is going to tuck them in at night? Who is going to feed them dinner? Being able to calmly answer their concerns in a positive fashion will make a tremendous difference in how they react to the actual event.

As they ask their questions, answer them in a clear and simple manner. "Let them ask all their questions, answer only the specific questions that they ask, and allow them to lead the discussion," says Dr. Streicher. "Don't add a lot of other things into the conversation simply because you've prepared some sort of speech in advance. Meet your child where your child is thinking."

In answering their questions, try to tune in to their feelings and validate them. Telling your child, "Looks like you're scared about this" lets the child know that you're really listening and respect her feelings. If she expresses negative feelings or you detect this, ask her directly to give you some suggestions for what might help her feel better.

Dr. Streicher explains that "children are usually fairly good reporters of what they need. If the requests are reasonable, try to honor them." For example, your child might say, "I'll miss you and be sad. Can I talk to you at work?" You might be able to schedule a time to call and check in with them and what they're doing, but be very clear about the parameters of the call. Tell your child ahead of time that "I'm going to call for five minutes at noon to see how you are." If you don't make the nature of the call clear and set some boundaries, you risk dealing with your child's meltdown when you try to hang up.

If your announcement is met by threats or temper tantrums, don't be swayed because if they see that their negative behavior causes you to change your plans they will make a mental note of that and give a repeat performance every time Mom isn't doing what they want.

Also, don't wait until the last possible moment to let them in on the fact that you're returning to work.

"The shift needs to be gradual," says Dr. Streicher. If they will be going to a new day-care center, take them there and show them where they will be, who they will be spending time with, and what types of activities are available. Consider spending half a day with your child at the day-care center. Similarly, if they will have a new nanny looking after them, be sure that you stay with them the first few times they are with the new person.

Also, because kids thrive on routine, make sure to detail for them exactly what their routine and your routine will be. Show them where you'll be working and discuss with them what you'll be doing.

When your child is older and in school, it is helpful to explain that your job now during the day will be to go to the office while her job is to go to school.

"Recognizing that they leave the home during the day is helpful in their gaining acceptance of the fact that you will now be doing that too," explains Dr. Streicher.

If your child has separation issues, try giving him transitional objects to help him with his anxiety during the day. For example, you might give him a small photograph of you to carry or something of yours that he knows is special to you to keep with him.

In the latter case, be sure to let the child know why the item means so much to you.

On your first few days back at work, talk to your child in the morning about what fun activities she will do during the day. Remember to be cheerful and optimistic when you leave so that your child has "permission" to be excited about her "new adventures" too. Give your child a quick hug and kiss and tell her goodbye. "It is critically important that you don't hang around and create long, drawn-out good-byes. If you linger too long, it will inadvertently send the message that there is a problem," says Dr. Streicher. "And, whatever you do, don't sneak out. This can create anxiety about the potential for future 'disappearing acts' by Mom."

Once you start work, make sure to spend time with your children every day. Call it your "special time" together or "making a date" with your child. Make it the first thing on your schedule and put it ahead of other activities you wouldn't think of missing. This will send the message to your child that he is still the highest priority in your life. Also, try to do thoughtful things that let your children know that even though you're not there physically, you are thinking about them, like leaving a little note or other inexpensive surprise in their lunch boxes for them to find. Finally, bring them to work on occasion so that they can see exactly where you are and what you're doing.

When Aubrey's children were young she would take them into her office on the weekend so they could visually understand where she was when she said she was at work and they could see that there were pictures of them all over her desk. She told them they could call her anytime they needed her and she would always answer the phone because if it was important to them it was important to her. She did all this when she was working for an employer who thought family was an unfortunate waste of time.

"My boss at the time restrained how much time I could take off to go to school plays. I tried to make up for my lack of flexibility in other ways," Aubrey said.

She's now a hospital administrator and she's employed the knowledge she gained working under family-unfriendly bosses to shape her policies.

"I insist employees go to their children's school events," she said.

Another mother said the best advice she can give is to spend the first ten minutes you come home completely devoted to your children. Play with them. Talk to them. Be focused on them.

"It's amazing how smoothly my evening went when I did that," she said. "Otherwise they'd fight to get my attention, get cranky, act out."

GETTING STARTED AGAIN

You've stayed home. You watched your baby learn to crawl, walk, and talk. Now you're moving on to the next phase of your life. What do you do?

Be realistic and give yourself at least six months to find a job. Don't stress out. Take it slow. Be methodical. It's hard to sprint from a sitting position.

Start small. Don't fall into the trap that your first job has to be your big job because you want to impress everyone who has asked you what you do for the past however many years it's been or because you feel pressure to make lots of money.

Your first job won't be your big job. Sorry to disappoint you. It'll probably be a step to the next-better job. Take that pressure off yourself and focus on getting any job that will look good on your résumé or put money in your pocket.

"When you want to come back you have to be ready to totally focus and give your employer everything. Otherwise you're giving women a bad reputation," one employer we talked to said.

He said former employees of his have called him a few months before they wanted to get back into the workforce and asked for advice. He was able to tell them what skills they needed to update, and they would be on his mind whenever he heard about an opening. So far, he has directed two former employees to new jobs because they reconnected with him and gave him plenty of lead time to help them. Women can do this themselves by contacting the human resources departments at companies they'd like to work for and asking for advice.

"When you want to go back to work you need to think of it as a months to yearlong process," he said.

HOMEWORK

Before you plunge into job hunting make sure you're employable. Get your skills updated.

Take a computer class. Don't try to weasel your way out of it. Look at the local community college course schedule or any continuing education outlet and sign up. No matter how little you think you'll be dealing with computers, you need to get your skills updated. A lot has changed in five or ten years. There are Internet search engines and e-mail, new software and technologies.

One employer said that she has nothing against women who have taken time off, but she'd more readily hire a recent college graduate than a woman who's been out of work for years because the graduate would have up-to-date skills.

"Technology changes so quickly that a woman who's out of work has to take classes to stay marketable," she said.

To figure out what classes will be the best use of your time she recommends reading trade journals and calling human resources personnel at companies you'd eventually like to work for and asking them what they're looking for. For example, she's looking for people who have taken a class in a new digital technology. She's sifted through hundreds of résumés and found only five with a relevant class listed on them. Those are the people she hired.

Susannah went to college before personal computers were all the rage. When she worked as vice president of a bank her assistant did all the typing. Yeah, we're all jealous of that.

She wasn't familiar with word processing programs. She didn't know how to type well—she did the hunt-and-peck thing. She wasn't real clear about the Internet. Truth be told, she's still grappling with her e-mail. She doesn't know how to send a message to two people at once. She recently learned how to do attachments, but is a little shaky.

She is a perfect example of someone who has to take a computer class. When she wants to go back to work, she'll need to know how to do all these things but she's adamant that she won't. She insisted to us that she knew everything that a job would require. So we put her to the test. We asked her to show us how to access LexisNexis, a fee-based Internet law library. She stared at us blankly and timidly sat down at her computer. She puttered around for a few minutes. She clicked and was able to access the Internet.

"I've heard of LexisNexis before. Are you sure it's on the Internet?" she asked.

She proved our point.

Another woman is an elementary school teacher who went back to work recently. She was shocked that there were computers in the classroom and she was expected to know how to navigate them. She had a steep learning curve and pulled quite a few all-nighters to get up to speed. Her nine year old was her teacher. Even with all her work, the six year olds in her class, who were basically born into computer use, were more computer literate.

If you really don't want to take a class, you probably can rely on your children to give you a tutorial. They are so tech savvy. At minimum, you need to know how to:

- use word-processing programs
- put together Power Points
- have a rudimentary understanding of Excel
- access search engines on the Internet
- send and receive e-mails
- attach documents and other files to e-mails
- access Web sites, including news- and work-related ones

YOUR NETWORK

Once you are on your way to being ready for employment, start asking around. Advertise to everyone you know that you're thinking about going back to work. By advertise, we don't mean do a hard sell, we mean bring it up casually in conversations. Doing that leads to discussion and referrals to other people who may be helpful to you.

Identify other women you know who have gone back to work or are successful. Ask them to lunch and pick their brains about the best way for you to go about finding a job. Find out what they did.

Still friendly with your old boss or coworkers? Schedule lunch. Give them your spiel. Spell out what you're looking for without asking for a job. Never put your contacts on the spot. During the lunch, you should ask about trends in your field. The knowledge will help you later during interviews.

Don't expect anything to happen right way. You're laying the groundwork. Something may pop up in a couple weeks or months. What you're doing is spreading out karma and there's no telling when good things will come back at you but they will. Be patient.

RÉSUMÉ

Your résumé is going to need lots of work. We say keep the dates off your résumé because dates draw the focus to how long you haven't been working instead of to your achievements. Of course, if they ask you tell them how long you have been out of the work-force and why you felt it was important to stay home, don't be ashamed of it. We're just saying there's no reason to broadcast it or make it the focus of your application. Also, keep the dates off your degrees and association memberships. Why should they know how old you are? We don't know about you, but we find as we age that information is for our eyes only.

"I'd like to know there was a reason they weren't working instead of the possibility that they didn't feel like it," one vice president of human resources at a technology firm said.

She went on to say that gaps in résumés are more acceptable now than they were a few years ago. Because of repeated downturns in the technology sector, for example, a lot of people have gaps in their work histories.

There's one place you should definitely use numbers. If you were in charge of a $2 million fund drive, put that on your résumé. If you were responsible for doing the financials for, say, the ballet, put that down as well as the amount of the budget.

List all your volunteer work.

If you renovated your house and basically served as general

contractor (and you probably did), put that down. It shows organizational and management skills.

If there's a big gap in your résumé, include strong professional and character references. This shows that you've kept in contact with your former boss and coworkers and have been active in your community.

Update the language in your résumé. Have a friend look at it. Let your sister take a gander at it. Print it out and read it out loud. You're more likely to catch mistakes this way.

Another good option is to seek career counseling. You can often get counseling for no cost through the YMCA and government agencies. These programs typically include career assessment, résumé writing, and interview skills.

Private coaching can also be good for those who have no idea what they want to do next professionally. Private coaching can be expensive. It's also more intensive. Coaches give you personality tests and perform in-depth interviews to figure out where your skill sets and interests lie.

INTERVIEWS

Prep for the interview by going to your local department store or mall. Look at the window displays to get an idea of what professional women are wearing nowadays.

Don't make the mistake Monica did. She hadn't been in a law office in three years when a relative asked her for help with a lawsuit. She agreed and enlisted a law school friend in the suit. The friend arranged a meeting with her and the relative in his downtown law office to discuss the case.

The day of the meeting she stood in front of her closet for a half an hour debating what to wear. She could wear a suit or dress pants and a blouse or a skirt. She was clueless about what would be appropriate. What does one wear to the office nowadays?

She was going to be late if she didn't choose something soon. She decided better to be overdressed than under so she settled on a nice blue suit with a strand of pearls.

As she waited in the lobby of the law firm a sense of dread came over her as she watched people walk in and out of the building. No one was wearing a suit. Her friend was wearing khakis and a blue striped button down shirt.

He looked Monica up and down and smiled.

"You're dressed up," he said.

Monica did have a clue that law offices had gotten more casual since she decided to stay home but she thought the casualness was more of a Friday thing. This was Wednesday.

Go on as many interviews as possible. They give you an opportunity to learn more current terms and language, which you can then pepper your conversation with on the next interview. You can also put the terms in your résumé, which makes it look more relevant.

When the interviewer asks you to tell him something about yourself, don't start with "I have two children." It sounds like that's what defines you and that's your priority in life. It may be true, but that's not what he wants to hear. It's better if you answer that question with all the other things you do. Then, if he asks you what you do in your spare time, you can mention your children.

During the interview, you should ask questions that will give you an idea how family friendly the employer is. Ask what they would expect you to do if your daughter is home sick with the chicken pox and you have a 10:00 A.M. presentation for clients. If they say they don't know, they've never had to deal with that before, we say run. Their answer shows that discussions of family issues aren't encouraged in the workplace.

If they say they'd expect you to come in, run. You know they're not going to be supportive. At least they were honest.

If they say they have arrangements with a day care that allows sick children or they have a babysitting service, you know you've found the right place. Ditto if they say they'd expect you to stay home with your sick child.

Be clear about what you need flexibility on. Do you want to be homeroom mom, which may mean being late some mornings? Do you want to pick your daughter up from dance class in the afternoons? Employers feel better with specifics rather than a blanket request for flexibility.

You need to ask questions regarding the juggling of your children and work even at the most family-friendly businesses because your manager is the one who chooses to recognize or ignore those policies. Your manager sets the tone of your working life so figure out where she's coming from.

Karen Hughes learned the importance of support in the workplace when she took an afternoon off work to go on a school field trip with her son. A staffer couldn't locate her to okay a press release and he told then Governor Bush that everything was done in the release except they couldn't locate Karen for the final approval. Bush replied, "That's what cell phones are for, call her."

His response validated Karen's choice to spend the afternoon with her son and kept her in the loop. That's the kind of support we all want.

GETTING IN THE DOOR

This is where your pride can't get in the way. You may have to take a job that is lower in skill, responsibility, and pay than the one you left. People who were your employees may now be your bosses. The horror!

Well, guess what, there are trade-offs when you take years off. All those people who stayed in the workforce when you left have been doing things, progressing. We know we wish they were in suspended animation all those years, but they weren't.

You should look at small companies. They typically value nontraditional skills or skills gained outside of the workplace more than bigger corporations.

Temp agencies are your friend. Oftentimes you'll get placed in a company that ends up hiring you. If nothing else, it's a good way to log current experience and start to feel comfortable in the workplace again.

Also check out the *Occupational Outlook Handbook* from the Labor Department's Bureau of Labor Statistics. It lists salary ranges and organizations for several professions. The Web site address is www.bls.gov/oco/home.htm.

Pat Harrison, president of the Corporation for Public Broadcasting, says get your foot in the door anywhere that treats you well. If you have talent and prove yourself capable, you'll rise. Pat hired one woman as a receptionist. She was obviously overqualified but she hadn't worked for a while. She said she was just interested in getting out of the house and loved answering phones and greeting people. Pat believed her.

The woman was very capable and within weeks started taking on other responsibilities. Pat kept telling her, your job is to answer phones and greet people; that's it. The woman continued to excel and a few months later Pat promoted her. She had no choice, the woman was the best candidate.

As long as you like your employer and know she's open to advancing you it doesn't matter what level you start a job at because you'll end up somewhere else quickly.

DON'T TAKE NO FOR AN ANSWER

In your search for a new job, you will meet lots of naysayers. They will take one look at your résumé and tell you you're toast in the nicest possible terms. Others may not be so respectful of your feelings. They may flat out tell you that you're wasting your time. If you believe every negative word sent your way in your job search, you are bound to get discouraged and quit.

Perseverance is the key. Accept advice in your job search, but don't accept anyone's discouraging words as final, no matter how authoritative they may appear to be.

Nancy didn't. In 1993, Nancy left a job at IBM to stay home with her children and run her own business. Despite her best efforts, the business never took off and by 2004 she was out looking for a job that offered a steady paycheck.

To get the job search going, Nancy met with a headhunter. She figured someone with experience in finding people jobs and who had a solid list of employers looking for qualified people was a surefire way for her to get the best job possible quickly.

She put together her résumé, highlighting her IBM experience and also hitting the high points she'd experienced in her own business. She handed the headhunter her résumé and waited for him to tick off the list of jobs she might like to pursue. He glanced at her résumé and then hit her with a verbal two by four. "With this résumé," he said, "you'll be lucky to find a job making $30,000 a year."

His opinion was that Nancy's lack of a W-2 the preceding ten years would be a big negative to prospective employers. He threw her a bone, however, by promising to do his best to help find her something provided she understood that her prospects for finding anything worthwhile were slim.

Instead of being discouraged, she was strangely hopeful. Years before she had landed her IBM job despite the odds. At her college campus, IBM advertised the position for an MBA. Nancy didn't have one, but she had the natural ability to sell. She snagged an interview, wowed the recruiters, and landed the job. Nancy thought something similar could happen this time around.

The headhunter sent her on an interview. When Nancy walked into the lobby she found a male applicant waiting for his interview at the exact same time. Both had been sent by the same headhunter. She called the headhunter. He apologized profusely for his mistake. Nancy had her suspicions. Rather than make a scene, however, she elected to take the high road and offered to be interviewed second.

The job was for a company that automates and outsources human resources. The ideal candidate for the position needed to successfully sell the company's services to new businesses. Nancy knew she could sell anyone under the table.

The company was interested in her after the first interview but she had to endure four more interviews stretched out over three months before they offered her the job.

"I really had to persevere. Interviewing has changed a lot in the last twenty years," she said.

Once the headhunter realized Nancy was a serious contender for the job he started working hard for her, no more double interviews. Nancy is part of the company's marketing team and she is able to do much of her work from home.

DON'T BE AFRAID TO QUIT

If it's not working, don't torture yourself. Quit.

We all want to try to salvage a bad situation. Our instinct is to blame ourselves and tough it out. That's good for a few weeks, but if it's really not working we have to cut the cord.

Cynthia is a well-respected editor. At the height of her career as news assignment editor, she quit. She took ten years off from the workforce. A friend finally lured her back. She was executive editor of one of the best papers in the country and she wanted Cynthia to head the science section. It was a dream job. The budget was generous. She was able to send one reporter to Antarctica for a story. Another went to South America.

Six months into the job, her friend was unceremoniously fired. The new executive editor wasn't so generous and didn't have much faith in Cynthia. He questioned every story she proposed for the section and cut her budget in half.

Cynthia quit. We're told we should stay in a job for a year no matter how bad it is because if we don't, we'll look like we're job hopping. But that's not true. If you have good reasons to quit, other employers will understand.

A week after Cynthia quit, she found another job at a magazine. That quickly deteriorated. She said most of the staff didn't have children and didn't understand her need to leave work at 5:30 P.M. most days. She quit after a month.

She found another job shortly after that was a good fit.

Her story flouts conventional wisdom and proves that you should remain true to your desire to balance work and family. Don't stay miserable in a miserable job. There's always a way out.

Before Karen Hughes became President Bush's right hand woman she was struggling with finding the balance between work and family. She was climbing up the career ladder when Phil Gramm's office hired her. It was a great step. Working for a U.S. senator is a high profile position. She didn't last a month. She quit after her supervisor asked her to bring in a note from the doctor's office to prove that she had brought her child to the doctor.

Imagine asking your child's doctor to write a note for you as well as your kid.

Karen is proof that things have a way of working out. In her next job with the Halcyon Group she split her time between home and office. Halcyon offered her the position with that flexibility because they knew having the right person was more important than having any person in the office from nine to five.

She was lured away from that job by the Texas Republican Party. They allowed her to work full time from home.

When she went to work for George Bush during his campaign for governor, she had to go back into the office. But during his presidential campaign, he permitted her to take her teenage son with her for five months on the road. She homeschooled him.

Karen says don't be afraid to ask for what you want on the front end. If you don't get it, you probably shouldn't take the job because it's unlikely to be a satisfying experience.

USING A HOBBY OR INTEREST AS A SPRINGBOARD BACK TO WORK

Do you enjoy creating handmade jewelry for friends or putting up yard signs for a political campaign? Sometimes you can turn a hobby or interest into a paying job.

Sascha used politics as a springboard back into work. Sascha quit her job at a high profile law firm and stayed home with her son for seven years. Once he started school, she got a little restless and started attending local Democratic Party meetings. When an opening for district judge came up, Sascha talked to party officials about backing her to run. They agreed. Within a year of getting involved, she was fund raising and shaking hands.

She narrowly lost the election. She was disappointed and exhausted, but the race raised her profile. The U.S. Attorney's Office called her and offered her a job. She took it.

"Working on a campaign gets you out there," Sascha says. "It put me in front of people I hadn't seen in years, which got me back on their radar when they were hiring."

Sascha works nine to five—unusual at most law firms. She says she's at the bottom rung of the U.S. Attorney's Office, but she doesn't mind. Maybe it's because she's older or maybe having a child has given her perspective, but she says she's not in a rush to prove herself. She's happy putting her mind to work. Though she does admit that she is contemplating another run for office.

Karen Hughes found politics to be much more accepting of nontraditional schedules and career paths than other professions. She was lured to work for the Republican Party of Texas when her future boss told her she could work from home. She could make her own hours as long as she got the job done. When she was a television reporter at a Dallas station, the job was a little more rigid. They required her to show up to the office every day and stay late. "I know there are jobs where people have to be in the office, but if it's not necessary then employers should be and I think are becoming more flexible about where and when employees get the job done," Karen said.

DEALING WITH A BEAN UP THE NOSE

So you're back at work. Things are different. You have kids at home who get sick and need you in emergency situations. You have a lot to prove to yourself, your boss, and your coworkers about whether or not you're up for the job. You feel like people are constantly evaluating what you put first, work or family. You feel guilty whenever you have to take a call from home or your child's school. How do you find the middle ground?

Debbie, who founded Flex-Time Lawyers, was in the middle of taking a deposition when her son's preschool called. During the arts and crafts portion of the day, her son had stuck a bean up his nose. When the teacher told him to blow out, he inhaled. The bean was lodged in his sinus passage. He needed a visit to the doctor pronto.

Debbie was huddled in the corner of the conference room on her cell phone saying significant things like bean, doctor, and preschool that her client and opposing counsel could hear. She could feel the back of her neck start to sweat. She hung up, apologized profusely, and said they'd have to reschedule the deposition. She ran out of the room beet red and perspiring.

At law offices, gossip about an embarrassing family emergency travels faster than news of who made partner. When Debbie arrived at work the next day, she could tell by the eruption of chatter as she passed that everyone in the office knew about her situation the day before. What to do? She felt humiliated and her future at the firm flashed before her eyes.

She decided to have a sense of humor about her situation and laugh it off. She made a lot of jokes with coworkers about it and there was plenty of opportunity to talk about the incident. By the time she walked into the office the following day, the story had morphed into her son getting stung by a bee and going into shock. Just about everybody found an excuse to drop by her office and check on her. "It was amazing. As soon as I joked and talked about it with someone, they'd have a story just like it. It was a great ice breaker," she said.

She said even a couple of the male partners at the firm also had stories about rushing out of a meeting to attend to a sick or injured child. It actually was one of those things that made Debbie stand out in a good way. She proved that she could deal well with a difficult situation.

BACK TO WORK HAZING

Another part of returning to work is the hazing you'll receive. For the first few months, you'll be low man on the totem pole. It doesn't matter if you're overqualified for the job and really in a lot of ways you're doing them a favor. What matters is they think you're beneath them because you haven't put the time in.

Rachel has a master's degree in science. She got a job as a teacher's aide because she needed to get out of the house and have more adult contact. Her first week on the job a teacher whose class she wasn't assigned to asked her to do something. Rachel said, "No problem, write the request down and put it in my box. I'll get to it later." The teacher was incensed. She thought Rachel was being rude and insubordinate. She told the principal and lodged a written complaint against Rachel, who didn't know anything about it until a couple months later when the principal reassigned her to work in another, less desirable classroom because of her problems with authority. Tread extra carefully until you understand the office politics.

Briana was a medical resident when she gave birth to her son. She took a few weeks off and then was back on the job. She worked twelve-hour shifts. Sometimes she had to stay overnight because she was on call. She was breast-feeding. Needless to say, she had to pump a few times during her shift. She tried to put a sign on the resident locker room when she was pumping so no one would come in. One of the other residents rebelled. He refused to honor her request. He complained to the chief resident.

The chief resident told Briana she couldn't breast pump in the locker room because it infringed on others' rights. He told her she could use the janitor's closet if she needed to "do that sort of thing." She complained. The other residents complained. Her bosses thought she was a troublemaker and decided not to offer her a position when she completed her training.

"Residents will eat their young to get a job offer. They knew they were knocking me out of the running by making a big deal over the pumping," she said.

Unlike the backstabbing passive-aggressive coworkers we've discussed, the resident in this case was directly aggressive. There will be times you'll find no knives in your back because you're under an all-out frontal assault. How can you deal with this?

- Identify the true source of the conflict. One industrial psychologist we spoke with suggests that the real problem may not always be readily apparent.
- Work conflicts usually come down to the most basic and personal things. The angry resident in question may have reacted the way he did because he was denied a privilege or simply because it was an inconvenience for him.
- Go to the individual and ask to talk about the problem.
- Don't just write off the person. Try to resolve the problem but understand that if your coworker's position is truly set in stone you may not reach a resolution.
- When discussing the issue, be empathetic. If the angry resident revealed that he felt inconvenienced by the arrangement, the female resident could have responded, "I totally understand that. I would probably feel that way too, but unfortunately it's something that I really

have to do which is why I'm so grateful that the hospital is helping me out this way." Acknowledging that
you understand where your coworker is coming from
may not solve the problem, but it will likely diffuse the
situation. Everyone likes to feel that, at the very least,
they are being heard.

- Keep in mind that many times the answer to your
problem is out of your and your supervisor's control.
Large institutions often have inflexible rules that don't
lend themselves to an easy solution.

YOUR STAY-AT-HOME FRIENDS

The friends you made when you stayed at home will have some
weird reactions to you when you go back to work. Some will resent or envy you. Some will be supportive. Some will feel like you
are making a statement against staying at home.

It's hard to navigate all the minefields, especially when you
have much less time to devote to these relationships. Know that
just as your circle of friends changed when you quit your job, it
will change when you go back to work. At first you'll make promises to get together as much as ever and you'll mean it, but things
will happen and some friends will fall by the wayside. Expect to
keep close to one, maybe two of them. It'll be lonely at times, but
you'll adapt like you've adapted to all the other changes.

Eva said her stay-at-home mom friends were actually angry at
her. That's right, angry. They felt like she had betrayed them by
going back to work. They said their husbands asked them why
they couldn't go back to work if she was. She was the litmus test
they were being held to. Remember, it's always the pioneer who
gets the arrows. After a few months they'll calm down.

STRATEGIES FOR KEEPING IN TOUCH

- Arrange to spend time with the mothers you befriended on the weekends. Set up weekend play dates with your kids.
- Make sure you don't just talk about work. They'll think you're bragging no matter what you say.
- In subtle and truthful ways, tell your friends what you envy about their situations. They are probably feeling a little insecure because in a sense they've been left behind. This kind of positive feedback will give them a boost.
- Remember their birthdays. Show extra kindness and thoughtfulness. This kind of goodwill goes a long way when you have to ask these mothers to take your kid home from the soccer game.

READJUSTING TO NOT BEING YOUR OWN BOSS

You've been your own CEO for the past few months or years. You knew what you had to accomplish and did it on your own schedule and in your own way. You woke up when you wanted, or more accurately, when your child wanted. You ate lunch when it was convenient. It didn't matter what you wore.

When you go back to work, you are no longer the ultimate authority in your life. It can chafe. It will feel unnatural. At times it will make you angry.

The first day Nellie went back to work for a marketing firm, she screwed up. She was sitting in a division meeting. Everyone was talking about a client's new campaign. The boss gave his opinion. She disagreed. She spoke up, which is a good thing, but then she tried to lead the meeting like she would a group of preschoolers. She spoke slowly, didn't use three-syllable words, and dominated the conversation. Her colleagues became very quiet. They waited for her to finish, then her boss ended the meeting.

"I was mortified. I forgot how to interact with adults," she said.

COMBATTING ANXIOUS FEELINGS

- Prior to starting your new job, enlist a few allies outside the workplace to act as lifelines in the event you have a "dumb question." When Monica's sister, Lisa, returned to work, she was concerned about using a computer. Her husband, an IT expert, agreed she could call him.
- Make sure you have competent child-care arrangements at home. Feeling that your children are safe in your absence will go a long way toward making you more effective on the job.
- Identify key people at work who would be willing to show you the ropes. It's helpful to be friendly with the receptionist and other members of the support staff. The receptionist knows who everyone is and where they are in the pecking order. No matter how important your new job is, you certainly won't wow your new bosses if you can't quite figure out how to use the telephone.
- Take advantage of the breaks offered by the company, but don't abuse them. You need to get up and stretch every once in a while. If you make sitting at your desk an endurance test, it will become one which you most likely will fail.

She apologized to her boss, promised it would never happen again, and was pretty quiet for the next few weeks until she learned how to play well with others.

Another friend had trouble adapting to an eight-hour work-day. She felt like she was in detention.

She came in to work at 9:00 A.M. and by 11:00 A.M. she was looking at the clock praying for lunch. She would take walks around the office to ward off some of her closed-in feelings. She contemplated taking up smoking because she would have a legitimate excuse to stand outside the building for a few minutes every couple of hours.

She didn't start smoking, but it took her about three months to become accustomed to sitting at her desk for hours on end.

If you feel like you're going crazy when you return to work or you're nervous about undertaking this new experience, relax. Most of us feel that way.

THE GOING-BACK-TO-WORK REDISTRIBUTION OF POWER

Your first job back will probably not pay as much as you used to make. This may hurt your ego. It will also be a trump card your husband may use, either unconsciously or extremely consciously. He may assume you should continue to take up the slack at home because you make less. Even if you work more hours than he does, it won't register as much as the salary. Plus, as we said before, men are creatures of habit. They like the status quo.

One woman forcibly rebalanced the division of labor when she went back to work. Every day she picked the children up from the babysitter, threw on her work-out clothes, handed the children over to her husband, and went to the gym for an hour. She did the enforced babysitter thing every day of the workweek. Her husband didn't like it, but what could he say, "How dare you leave me alone with my children, my flesh and blood?"

We're not advocating this exactly. We do think it's important to carve out time for yourself though, and in order to do that you'll have to shift some more responsibility to your husband. We'd recommend talking to him about it first.

Before you do talk to him, get the skinny on what the men think.

"I'm at work, if she's at home why shouldn't she start dinner and play with the children," one man said.

In fact, it annoys him that his wife, who works full time but not as many hours as he does, expects him to make dinner a couple times a week and play with the children when he gets home. He said that she's being juvenile, almost like another child, to demand he fulfill her needs without thinking of his.

"When I get home I need an hour or two to unwind. Playing with the children isn't unwinding. I have no problem spending time with them on the weekends. I take them to story hour. I have a problem when she thrusts them on me like it's some sort of duty," he said.

Another man was adamant he wasn't being chauvinistic, quite the contrary, he was being socialistic. He's a stockbroker. She's a social worker.

"We divide labor equally. I work and make money. She works a little. She should cook and watch the kids. That's how it should work in a fair world," he said. "Instead this whole women's movement thing has empowered women and given men less and less. If I tell her I worked a full day, so she should do the dishes, I'm a jerk."

Before you confront your husband for behavior similar to that of the men discussed above, try diplomacy. Explain to your husband what your responsibilities are each day and remind him what the definition of partner is—the kind of relationship where you help each other out. After you have been working a few months, a lot of the reentry problems will go away on their own because your job will no longer be new. It will be part of the routine, and we know men like the routine.

9
Career Counseling

When You Need a Change

You know you want to go back to work but there's no way you want to go back to what you left behind.

A lot of the women we talked to had a career crisis after they had kids. Taking a couple years off to spend with your children gives you time to reexamine your life and what makes you happy. You realize that the thing you studied to be in college and then became wasn't what you thought it would be or that you've changed and it's no longer what you want.

We call it the lawyer syndrome. We're picking on lawyers because we'd say 99 percent of the women we interviewed who practiced law and took time off didn't want to go back to practicing. Most people who go to law school don't know what being a lawyer involves. They see the TV shows, think it sounds good (I'm an attorney), promises job security, and gives them another three years in school to figure things out. Then reality hits. They find themselves in jobs that take up most of their lives and they hate it.

Other careers fit this description—lots of other careers. Take journalism—after a few years of working at a newspaper and writing versions of the same story several times a year J.C. began to loath it. Most of the journalism majors she graduated college with are no longer in journalism, or they're desperate to get out of it.

Many women in scientific research get out of it when they have families. Recording and analyzing scientific results that are time sensitive isn't conducive to a twenty-hour-per-week schedule. Plus, science is evolving so rapidly that if you take a couple years off your knowledge base is dated.

Use the time at home to plan for your next career. Tammy went back to school. She tried her hand at writing—didn't pay enough. She worked for her husband. She sampled lots of different careers while her children were little. When she was ready to go back to work full time, she knew what she wanted to do and had some experience to back her up. She ended up working with her husband in his public relations firm.

That's what we're advocating. While you're home you have an opportunity to try what you love nearly risk free. Most people don't get this chance. Take advantage of it.

As Pat Harrison, president of the Corporation for Public Broadcasting, wisely advised, "Give yourself at home the job of preparing for the job you're going to have someday."

If you've always wanted to be a tennis pro, test drive it. Vocation Vacations is a Portland, Oregon, company that pairs you with experts in fifty fields ranging from doggy day care owner to cowboy boot maker. The company arranges for you to shadow the expert in his or her job for a few days.

IT'S THE CULTURE, STUPID

As successful women bail out of the workforce to care for their children, at least some corporate leaders have taken a sharp turn inward to find out why.

In 1992, Deloitte & Touche, a business consulting firm, internally investigated why it was hemorrhaging so many qualified women from its ranks. The company's chairman and CEO at the time, J. Michael Cook, rounded up the firm's best and brightest to drill down on the underlying causes of these losses, stanch the bleeding, and prescribe long-term remedies like Personal Pursuits, a program that provides training, mentoring, and career coaching to stay-at-home moms who used to work for the firm.

Deloitte today enjoys less female turnover, more women partners, and unprecedented profitability. In the natural order of corporate cultures, D&T made all the right moves, to the mutual benefit of the company and its talent pool.

Other companies, like Tom's of Maine, a natural products company, and Athleta Corp., a women's sports apparel company, have also broken the code. It doesn't take a rocket scientist to figure out that an investment in their personnel has been squandered if their highly trained women are out the door just as they are reaching their more productive years with the organization. Some law firms, hardly considered a wellspring of progressive management innovations, offer part-time tracks to partnership. Not that it's a parade as yet, but a respectable number of corporations offer employees child care, job sharing arrangements, and flexible schedules.

BENEFITS TO LOOK FOR BEFORE SIGNING ON

- Flexible hours—Ask your potential coworkers how flexible the hours are.
- Sick policy—If your child suddenly becomes ill at school and you need to leave work to take her to the doctor, will this count against your own sick leave or will it apply to vacation days? Instead of asking this during an interview, ask if the company has any written policies you could take a look at later.
- Vocation and holidays—Not every company follows the same holiday and vacation schedule. Monica's sister, for example, worked for several years for a French telecommunications company, which shut down the last two weeks of December with full pay to its employees. Some employers let you have President's Day off but not Columbus Day. Find out the vacation and holiday schedule for any prospective employer and compare it to your children's school schedule. If you see too much conflict between the two, the job might not be worth it.
- Insurance—Does it cover just you or your entire family? How much will you have to contribute to the premium payments? How much is the deductible? Some insurance policies have such high deductibles for each family member that they really amount to no more than catastrophic coverage.

GOING BACK TO SCHOOL

This is it. You can get a degree. Any degree you want. So what do you want? Think hard about what you might want to do.

Interview other people doing it. See a career counselor. Shadow someone for a day.

Our friend Olivia went back to school to get a teaching degree specializing in math. Before she did, she substitute taught for a year. She taught a spectrum of grades and subjects. The experience allowed her to hone her focus to seventh grade—we can't believe it, but middle schoolers were her favorite group. Apparently, they're smart, articulate, and still malleable. We guess they're different at school.

She discovered that she made her best connections with kids in math. She said it's a subject that lots of students are intimidated by and she knew how to break it down for them. It was also her favorite subject when she was in school.

Olivia used to be a lawyer, but like so many attorneys she found the work tedious and boring. What did we tell you? It's the lawyer syndrome. She went to law school because she didn't know what she wanted to do after graduating college. Getting a law degree seemed like a safe and secure professional path. Her parents pushed her to do it as well.

She was offered a job at a good firm. That's when her problems began. She was miserable, but thought that's the way work works. When she stayed home with her daughter she realized how much she loathed her job. She talked to other mothers who had loved what they did and realized she needed to change.

Her decision to become a teacher came with sacrifices. Her salary is less than half of what it was as a lawyer. When she tells people she looks forward to working with preteens everyday, they look at her like she has had a nervous breakdown. When she says, "I'm a teacher," it doesn't have the same cachet as "I'm a lawyer."

The benefits are she loves what she does now. Her hours are the same as her children's and she has summers off. Plus, at the end of each day she feels like she has accomplished something real and tangible.

Another friend who was trained as a nurse, Natalie, went to medical school. You heard us right, medical school. She has a little boy and she's in medical school. We didn't know how she balanced everything until we sat down and asked her or tried to ask her. Trying to schedule time to interview her became an exercise in the absurd.

"Do you have a free half hour in the next couple of weeks?" we asked.

"No."

"In the next month?"

"I have fifteen minutes in three weeks."

"What about after school?"

"I'm picking up Todd."

"What about lunch? Can we talk during lunch?"

"I don't take lunch."

"You don't eat."

"I eat and study. I need that time."

We ended up meeting at a Chuck E. Cheese on a Saturday afternoon. Our first question was, "Why do you do med school?"

"Because I love it," she said.

She loves school and loves her son, so she makes it work. Her son spends days at Natalie's mother's house. A lot of times her mother cooks dinners for Natalie to take home to her husband. Other times, Natalie's husband cooks. When all else fails, they order Chinese.

Natalie spends three hours playing with her son before she puts him to bed. She studies until midnight and gets up at 6:00 A.M. to start all over again. There's not a lot of sleep built into the schedule, but Natalie says she makes up some sleep on the weekend. She is the most anal retentive person out there. So when she says she spends three hours with her son and five hours studying, it really is that amount of time, not a minute more or less.

Her husband does the dishes, vacuums, and does a lot of the parenting on the weekends. He even planned their son's birthday party and made a cake decorated with Sponge Bob. He has had to learn to cook and make Todd's lunch. Natalie tells us about the cold pizza in brown paper bags that he sends him to school with. She is in charge of laundry.

"He's not always happy about picking up so much of the work. At times he says he feels like a single parent, but he understands what I'm doing is important," she says.

They took out a second mortgage on their home to pay for Natalie's education. They're in this together emotionally and financially. She has a year left of school and then there's residency and internships.

"Is it all worth it?" we ask her as she details the plan for the next four years of her life, which sounds much like what she does now but worse.

"Absolutely," she says.

Elsa took the slow approach to getting her college degree. She took ten years to earn her bachelor's degree. Part of the reason it took her so long was because she couldn't take more than two classes a semester. She didn't have the child care. The other part of the reason was that taking classes allowed her to get out of the house and use her brain. She enjoyed her education. She liked the idea of taking it slow and figuring out what she wanted to do along the way, and she knew she didn't want to go back to work until her youngest child started kindergarten. The way her children are spaced she would have to stay home for ten years from the start of the oldest child to the kindergarten of the youngest.

If you don't have a university in your town that focuses on your area of interest, you could consider commuting to a college an hour or so away. Just make sure your classes are all on the same day or in two days. You might also consider enrolling in an executive program in which there are intensive classes over the weekend or during a two-week period for eight hours a day. There are also online universities to consider, although these are usually very expensive. We recommend talking to a counselor at your local college or even high school about your options.

INTERNSHIPS

You're never too old to work for free. We know you're rolling your eyes and thinking you'll never do that, but internships are indeed worthwhile.

You get a real sense what the career you're thinking about is like. You meet valuable contacts and you see what it's going to take to get to where you want to be.

Our friend Jolie wanted to work in the movies. She applied for and got an internship working for a production company. She worked on a movie and realized a couple things. She didn't want to work on the film set. Working on the set involves a lot of standing around and waiting for fifteen to eighteen hours a day while getting spontaneously yelled at because you're the least important person there (aka scapegoat).

It wasn't a practical schedule for a mom who has to pick up her children at a certain hour, put them to bed by eight, and see her little ones on a regular basis. It's also nearly impossible to parent when there are large chunks of the day you aren't allowed to use your cell phone because the movie is filming. Ambient noise like ringing cell phones is a death-by-catty-stares offense.

After one too many babysitter emergencies, Jolie asked to be transferred off the set. She was sent to the art department. It was a godsend.

Designing sets is a creative process. Sticking to the budget as you build the sets is a whole different creative process. She loved scrounging around at garage sales for the perfect dumpy couch for a fraternity house set. She adored the challenge of finding a cheap, rentable, stuffed grizzly bear. She loved it, and she would've never known that she wanted to do it if she hadn't done the internship. She wouldn't have even known there was a job out there like set designer.

The contacts she made during the internship enabled her to get other jobs and work her way up in the industry. Film professionals are always searching for people who are dependable, flexible with hours, and able to do jobs ranging from two days to three months in length. Sound like a job for a stay-at-home mom to you?

Erin nearly said no to an internship that turned into a job. She wrote several freelance articles and built up a substantial portfolio. On a whim she sent her résumé and clips in to a newspaper for a job. The recruiter called and offered her an internship. It was paid and lasted for twelve weeks but the recruiter said it absolutely wouldn't lead to a full-time position. Erin said no. She thought the recruiter had clearly spelled out that it was a dead-end proposition and she was a thirty-five-year-old woman. She felt above scrambling around an office getting coffee.

The next day the recruiter called Erin back and told her she should reconsider and take the position.

"It was funny. We were having this conversation where she didn't promise anything but I could tell in her tone that there might be a possible job after the internship. It was a wink-wink, nudge-nudge thing," she said.

Erin took the internship and worked her butt off. She sucked up her pride and smiled her way through working alongside eighteen-year-olds writing obits and fluffy weather features. Major dailies are devoted to weather stories. Maybe it's the heavy senior citizen subscriber base, but you're not a journalist until you've written at least one weather story.

In addition to the nonchallenging assignments Erin endured the eighteen-year-olds saying things like "You're that old!" and "You're a mother? What are you doing here?" For all her struggles and good work, Erin was offered a job as a reporter and took it.

Even if they say there's absolutely no way they'll hire you after the internship, you never know. They might. What do you have to lose by trying it?

Another friend, Abby, was slave labor for a year at Nickelodeon, the kid's television station. She wrote for a cartoon as an intern for what amounted to $2 an hour—she calculated it after the year was done. She was the first in the office and the last to leave. She learned the meaning of call backs—when you reference a joke again later in the episode—and the pacing of a half-hour television show. She even received a story credit on one show, which means she thought up the episode's idea. In television writing, you may create the plot of the show but at least five other people are involved in writing the whole episode. It's a very communal way of working.

After the year was done, Abby wasn't hired on. The staff and her supervisor liked her, but they didn't have a place for her. Abby was disheartened. At thirty-six she had felt too old to do the internship in the first place, and for it not to have resulted in a job was a little more than she could bear. She became depressed. She decided to go back to doing her stay-at-home mom duties while she regrouped. Nickelodeon called her six months later to offer her a job as an assistant to the head writer on another television show. She accepted. She plans to work her way up the ranks.

"It's not easy to break into a new career. I had to swallow a lot of my pride to do it. I'm glad I did," she said.

HOW TO FIND AN INTERNSHIP

- Identify the industry you're interested in working in, for example, film, advertising, education.
- Research what companies are located in your city or nearby.
- Call them or visit their Web sites to see if they offer a formal internship program.
- If they don't offer a program, figure out how many hours a week you could devote to working for a company for free for two months.
- Once you calculate the number of hours and determine when you could be available, approach a company with an offer of free work for two months.
- Don't be discouraged if the first one turns you down. Hone your pitch and try again.

OTHER INTERNSHIP RESOURCES

- Call your local community college career services offices. Typically they work with students and the community at large. They have a large database of internships.
- Try professional organizations for the field you're interested in.
- Hire a professional career counselor. This is the most expensive route, but can be useful.
- Try one of the annual internship directories like *Peterson's Internships 2005* or *The Internship Bible, 2005*.

APPRENTICESHIPS

An apprentice? Sounds like an indentured servant or maybe a position that requires a utility belt, gimme cap, and a polyester jumpsuit with "Arlene" stitched on the pocket. Hardly the traditional comeback trail, but more women are finding their way into what was one of those last male bastions—the trades. Think about it—you can be your own boss, make your own hours, and at the end of the day you can point to something you did that's real rather than a bunch of papers you've moved from one side of the desk to another.

These professions aren't walk-ons. They require training, but they combine the school with work so you're making money while you're learning. Often your sponsor or employer will pick up the cost of the program. Rarely will you be asked to pay. But err on the safe side and carefully read the fine print in any contract you sign. You may be required to foot the bill for books and tools—it's good to figure that out before you start. If you leave the program early you might have to pay for the education you already received. Make sure you understand all the possible costs before you begin.

The big problem with apprenticeships is it can be difficult to find a position. At times there are waiting lists of qualified people angling to get a spot. Sometimes there's a brother-in-law system in effect—you know, where they hire people they know or are related to. Don't be discouraged if it takes you awhile to land a slot. With perseverance you can do it.

Sheila managed an architectural office for seven years. She quit after the birth of her first child. As she dealt with postpartum depression and diaper rash, she also went through a career crisis.

"I was obsessing about work. I didn't know I hated it as much as I did until I quit. I had to find something else to do," she said.

Unlike a lot of us, she didn't harbor any hidden desires to write or design clothes. She had no idea what she wanted to do. She only knew what she didn't want—a boss, set office hours, and high heels. She hates high heels. She's five feet, eight inches tall, she doesn't need them.

She scouted around for a couple years. She read *What Color Is Your Parachute?* She went to a career counselor who told her she'd make a good mortician—she begs to differ. She was stumped. It was her father who suggested she try plumbing. He owns a plumbing business, which he'd love to pass down to her eventually. He proposed that they work together until he retires. He'd train her and offer her flexible hours.

She was hesitant at first. She'd have to put in five years of education and on-the-job training and she'd be a plumber. "Hi, I'm Sheila and I'm a plumber," wasn't something she'd ever thought she'd say. Though she's tall, she's not a manly woman; she couldn't picture herself hauling around a toolbox and driving around in a van with a wrench decal on the side.

Months of her father's nagging and her husband's encouragement convinced her to try it. She liked the technical parts of school and she loved the idea of working up to owning her own business. Another plus, women make the majority of financial decisions in the household and they like dealing with other women. Sheila's being by her father's side increased business.

Sheila completed her third year of her apprenticeship. Her son is in second grade. Most days she picks him up from school, barring a plumbing crisis.

"I was lucky. My dad made it easy for me," she said.

There are a lot of owners of businesses like Sheila's dad. They're ten years or so away from retirement and their children have no interest in taking over the business. They are hunting for someone to buy the business from them. Women are increasingly proving themselves successful entrepreneurs and are moving into nontraditional fields.

Rebecca, a former teacher, had been home for five years with her two children. She knew she didn't want to go back to the high school science lab and she started casting about for something to do. She took a couple woodworking classes and found her calling.

She convinced her teacher to take her on as an apprentice for a three-year term. She learned how to make old-fashioned dressers and bed sets without nails or glue. She learned how to carve ornate designs, take full advantage of a wood's grain, and do antique reproductions.

She worked five hours a day at her teacher's workshop and took certain pieces home with her. When her children went to sleep, she went to the garage, where she set up a workshop and continued to practice.

Her teacher specializes in high-end commissioned furniture. He was doing so well that he needed more workers to help expand his business. As Rebecca became more skilled, he asked her to take on some of his commissions. The relationship has worked beautifully. Rebecca finished her three-year apprenticeship and is now employed at the shop.

Paige went off the healthy living deep end when she stayed home with her four children. Four children can wreak havoc on the body and she was determined to lose her baby weight. She tried organic, vegetarian, and vegan diets. They were too lightweight for her. Then she discovered macrobiotic cooking—you know, the food philosophy where you shouldn't eat tomatoes, spinach, or eggplant because they are considered too yin. Gwyneth Paltrow and Madonna are fans. Paige became a fanatic.

She bought five macrobiotic cookbooks. She enrolled in classes. She had stumbled onto her passion.

She got a macrobiotic cooking certification, and then she found an experienced macrobiotic chef to apprentice with for two years.

The chef catered to wealthy individuals who wanted to get healthy—making tasty organic, nondairy, whole grain dishes ain't easy or cheap. Paige helped her prepare meals for more than thirty clients daily. She learned a lot about varying cooking, creating recipes, and pleasing clients.

After her two-year apprenticeship she snagged a job creating

RESOURCES FOR APPRENTICESHIPS

- The U.S. Department of Labor Employment and Training Administration lists opportunities on its Web site, www.do-leta.gov.
- Wider Opportunities for Women lists on its Web site nontraditional job and apprenticeship opportunities for women, www.work4women.org.
- Home Builders Institute lists on-the-job training opportunities in home construction, www.hbi.org.
- Check with your local chamber of commerce. Oftentimes they have connections or leads on what apprentice opportunities are available in your community.
- Interested in becoming an electrician? Check out the National Joint Apprenticeship and Training Committee, www.njatc.org or the National Brotherhood of Electrical Workers, www.ibew.org.

menus for a macrobiotic restaurant and is building up her own private client base. She's also experimenting with a nondairy no-refined-sugar ice cream that actually tastes good. If it works, she'll get a license for it and may try to partner with a large food company.

USING YOUR DEGREE IN A DIFFERENT WAY

Our lawyer friend, Debbie, knew she didn't want to practice law like she did before she had children. She worked part time for a couple of years at a law firm. Then she started a monthly group for lawyers that met to discuss work and life balance, Flex-Time Lawyers.

At the first meeting, the room was packed. She knew she was on to something. She developed the group further and opened chapters in other cities. The meetings received a lot of national attention. There were write-ups in the *New York Times* and *USA Today.* Her law firm supported her and encouraged her to accept public speaking engagements while she decreased her case load.

While Debbie still works part time at the firm, her main duties are public speaking and consulting with other law firms about how to make them more female friendly.

She says that more women should use their degrees and skills in different ways rather than abandon them altogether.

"It's great to explore your creative side, but you spend years getting an education and honing your skills. You should use them," she said.

A friend who was trained as a doctor and decided she could live without treating another patient has put her medical degree to use in two different ways. She's a medical expert for a local news program. She makes weekly two-minute appearances on the noon broadcast and covers drugs, health concerns, and diseases that have been in the news.

She also works for a consulting firm that writes reports for hospitals and other health-care institutions about medical devices. The firm pays experts like her to evaluate devices and give their opinion about how useful they are and whether or not it would be a good investment to buy them.

Claudia had a teaching degree and a master's in social work. After staying home with her children for five years she decided she didn't want to go back into a classroom or work for social services. She wanted more autonomy and creativity.

She saw an article in the paper about an increase in teenage dropout rates in high school due to financial pressures. Many kids quit high school to help support their parents. Others were now parents themselves and quit to provide for their children. From that article she developed an idea that she thought could help these teenagers.

Over two years, she applied for several grants and talked county and state officials into helping fund her program, which is basically a flex-time high school. If students work days, they can attend class at night and vice versa. If weekends are the best time for them to learn, classes are also available then. In addition to educational instruction, teachers provide career and life skills counseling.

EVALUATING YOUR EDUCATIONAL BACKGROUND

- Take your résumé and copies of your college transcript to a human resources specialist in the field you think you might like to pursue. Ask her to suggest any courses or degree programs you should take in order to increase your chance for employment in that field.
- If you're certain that you will need another degree in order to follow a particular career path, make an appointment with a college counselor. Bring copies of your transcripts to the meeting and ask her to give you some idea as to the types of courses and length of time it would take to pursue a degree.
- If you're not sure what sort of new career you might like, ask the counselor to suggest a few options based on the degree or courses you've already taken.
- Talk to a human resources employee at a company you want to work for, explain your experience and education, and ask for suggestions concerning classes you should take to make yourself marketable.

10
Entrepreneurs

True Stories

Some women change careers. Some women build empires. Have you heard of Pea in the Pod or Naissance? They're maternity clothing companies created by fed-up fashion-forward moms. And here's the best part, they're tallying annual revenue in the millions. Not bad for hormonally challenged females.

We talked to dozens of women who have succeeded in starting their own businesses. We'll discuss first steps you should take if you're considering such a move, as well as financing considerations.

We're not going to lie to you. Running your own business ain't easy. Then again, neither is marriage nor child-rearing.

The female entrepreneurs we've talked to listed the positives as:

- You're the boss. You make your own hours.
- You can ramp up the business when the kids go to school.

- You're putting your college education to work.
- You're making your own money.
- You're devoting your time to an activity you love.
- No one can lay you off.
- You can take vacations whenever you want.
- Depending on their age, your kids can help and learn something about business.
- You're doing something you never thought you could. Your confidence soars.
- You can attend your child's soccer game and your boss can't yell at you.
- You're showing your children a positive role model.

The negatives are:

- You're the boss. All the responsibility falls on your shoulders.
- Underfunding is common when you first start a business or want to expand.
- Your partner might look at your new company as a cute hobby rather than a job and may not give you the additional help you need to make it a success.
- You may fail.
- Your children may resent the long hours you're working.
- You'll be spending less time with your children.

That said, the women we talked to by and large are glad they started their own businesses. And they're part of a nationwide trend. The number of women-owned firms grew by 11.1 percent to 10.1 million from 1997 to 2002, more than 1.5 times the rate of all privately held businesses, according to the Center for Women's Business Research. Firms that are 50 percent or more female-owned account for a whopping 46 percent of all privately held U.S. firms. And women aren't only starting more firms, they're growing them at a rapid clip. From 1997 to 2002, sales at women-owned businesses rose by 32 percent versus 24 percent for all private businesses.

Many female entrepreneurs are jumping into fields not traditionally populated by women. Between 1997 and 2002, the number of female-owned businesses in construction jumped by 36 percent, those in agricultural science by 27 percent, and those in public utilities climbed by 24 percent.

"There's no longer a stigma attached to a woman being an entrepreneur and taking a risk," says Carrie, a financial planner.

Carrie worked at Fidelity before she took three years off to spend time with her daughter. When her daughter started nursery school, she created her own financial consulting firm. She says the consulting business has blossomed.

"My specialty is high net worth women. There are a lot of us out there and many feel more comfortable talking to another woman," Carrie says.

COMING UP WITH AN IDEA

Coming up with an idea for a viable business can be as easy as being pregnant. A lot of female entrepreneurs are inspired by their pregnancy and parenting experiences. Some get motivated by their former professions or hobbies. The important thing is not to talk yourself down before you even begin.

It's so typical for us to dismiss a brilliant idea because it is our own. Dare to trust yourself and agree not to discount anything until you've researched its plausibility.

Jennifer Noonan, a former public relations executive, hated

the maternity clothes available during her pregnancy. She didn't like polyester blends. She didn't like the plastic hangers, fluorescent lighting, and industrial carpet that decorated most maternity stores.

"Do they think pregnant women have lost their joy of shopping?" she asked.

It was her husband who pushed her to do something with her idea. They drove by a new mall that was opening soon in their neighborhood and he suggested she open a maternity store done in her image. He dared her and she accepted.

She signed a ten-year lease and spent more than $100,000 renovating the store, buying inventory, and designing her own clothes. She dipped into her family savings to fund the first year of operations.

The first month went by and there was only a small trickle of people into the store. Jennifer tried to attract attention with a risqué window display. She made a deerskin floor-length maternity halter dress. Its price tag was $3,000.

"I didn't expect anyone to buy it. It was meant to start people talking," Jennifer says.

Two days went by and no one went into the store. Jennifer was standing in line at a nearby baby clothes store and the two women in front of her were talking about what stores in the mall would close. They said in unison the maternity clothes store—they had never seen anything so tacky. Jennifer felt like she was punched in the gut. The comments made her physically ill.

"Even though I was upset I never doubted my concept. I thought, 'I have to move to closer to the city, where they'll get this,'" she says.

Jennifer did move the store a couple of months later, but before she did she sold the $3,000 dress to a fashion stylist who worked for Jada Pinkett Smith, who wore the dress in a *Vogue* photo shoot.

"It just goes to show, you should trust your instincts," Jennifer says.

Jennifer's new location was on Melrose Avenue in downtown Los Angeles. Naissance on Melrose is light and airy with blond wood floors and gold velvet curtains. There are no sailor dresses. Jennifer designs many of the clothes, which are form-fitting and echo her regular outfits—jean skirts, halter tops, funky T-shirts, and cargo pants. California cool. She even sells her designs wholesale to other maternity stores across the country. She says she generates about $3 million a year in revenue.

Jennifer isn't the only woman to cash in on her motherhood frustrations.

Beth Besner got the idea for her business after her son threw his plate like a Frisbee after eating at one too many restaurants.

"Every mother knows the peril she's in whenever she takes her child out to eat," Beth says.

Beth, who practiced bankruptcy law, created the Table Topper, a disposable placemat that adheres to restaurant tables so that toddlers can eat on a clean, stable surface.

The path from idea to viable product was fraught with disappointment, regrouping, and inventiveness. Initially the placemat was made of rubber with suction cups on the bottom. It would've cost $30,000 to make a mold for the first one. That was out of Beth's price range. Discouraged, she dropped the idea for a couple of months. She racked her brain for another way to make the placemat. In the bathroom one day she was looking at the maxipad box, she opened up a pad, ran into the kitchen, stuck it on the table, and pulled it up. The adhesive left no mark on the wood and it was strong enough that it wouldn't be dislodged by a toddler's little hands. Perfect. She found a cheaper and accessible way to make the placemat.

Had she given up at the first sign of an obstacle, the Table Topper wouldn't be carried in Toys R Us, lots of grocery stores, and Wal-Mart. There wouldn't be a product.

She created a company called Neat Solutions. Using her legal expertise, she patented the disposable placemat and negotiated contracts for its manufacture and distribution. The company has also developed another product, the Potty Topper, a disposable sheet that adheres to public toilets. She got the inspiration from the mess her toddler made with the slippery paper toilet seat covers in public restrooms.

"It started out really small. I was frustrated whenever I took my son out to eat or to a public toilet, and I knew other mothers were frustrated, too. I created Table Topper and Potty Topper because I needed them, but I didn't expect them to sell as well as they have."

Today sales are more than six figures a year.

"You can't go into a business thinking that you'll become rich. You have to believe in or love what you're doing. From idea to money-making company took years. If I didn't love doing this, I would've stopped long before the idea became successful," Beth says.

Laura, a spokeswoman for a clothing designer in New York, plucked inspiration from discomfort to start her business. Her infant was colicky for three months straight in the dead of winter. Laura was with him twenty-four hours a day in her apartment as he cried hysterically. It was too cold to take him outside and she was going insane. Her husband suggested they take a road trip down to Florida because if they were in a warm climate they could at least take him outside to cry.

"Everyone thought we were crazy for taking a twenty-hour

drive down to Florida with a crying infant. But you know what? As soon as we got into the car he stopped crying," Laura says.

Laura and her husband started joking around about the soothing effects of a baby road trip. Along the ride, the joke morphed into a video idea and a business plan. For the next week, while they were in Florida, they took turns holding the baby and writing the plan.

"I always had ideas for businesses but I never did them. Having a child inspired me to think in a different way and to take the next step," Laura says. "After what I went through in labor, I had plenty of confidence and motivation to make things better for my son."

As soon as they got back from Florida, Laura did focus groups and pored over other infant videos on the market.

She made a list of everything she liked and didn't like. There are so many products out there she knew hers had to stand out. She created an idea for a video series that was educational and included real footage of circuses, beaches, and jungles as well as puppets.

Ruth's business idea came straight from her former career. Before she had a son, and took three years off to stay at home with him, she worked as a press liaison for a food manufacturer. As soon as her son started nursery school, she launched her own public relations firm.

"Public relations is an easier field to go back into than, say, corporate law. I always knew I could get another job, but what I wanted was freedom," Ruth said. "My approach was risky but I thought if I didn't do this now I never would."

She funded a lot of her expenses with credit cards.

"Thank god my husband was supportive," she says. "There were many times when I thought this was a stupid idea and I should get a real job, but he made me stick it out."

Ruth said the biggest difference she's seen between successful entrepreneurs and people who fail is how long people stick it out.

"It took three years before I started to make a profit. If I quit after the second year I would've never known that I could make this work."

In five years, Ruth has signed many big names and now has twelve employees.

EDUCATING YOURSELF

Many of the entrepreneurs we talked to had never gone to business school, worked a spreadsheet, or kept track of accounts receivable. That's right, they didn't know a lot about what they were getting into. The successful ones took a few business classes, did tons of market research, and relied on friends and professors for reality checks concerning their ideas.

Sandy used a lot of unconventional methods to research her business. The mother of five decided she wanted to start a yoga studio. She figured out from talking to people at yoga studios across the country that the main practitioners of yoga are other mothers. She then looked at Little League enrollment statistics to pinpoint the biggest population of mothers in the Fort Lauderdale and Boca Raton area. She looked for a location near other stores that mothers go to, like Starbucks, bookstores, and local restaurants.

"That way, when they're going about their normal routine they'll happen upon us," Sandy says. "One restaurant near us has a line out the door most weekends. While those people are waiting they usually walk around the area and it's a perfect time for them to see we're here."

Sandy also interviewed other businesses to figure out what the down and busy times are, so she could better predict cash flow.

Even with all her careful planning some things didn't go off well. The cash register and credit card machine didn't work for the first week of business. She ended up using a shoe box full of cash until they were fixed. The prenatal yoga class failed despite women expressing interest in it. However, the children's yoga classes and birthday parties have taken off.

"You can't predict why one thing works and the other doesn't. You have to be observant enough to cut the things that don't work and nurture those that do," Sandy says.

After taking a couple of years off from her psychology practice to stay home with her children, Tina decided to relaunch a failed family business of making and selling relishes. Tina launched her business with the $5,000 she was planning to spend on a family vacation. She used $4,000 of it to convert her home kitchen into commercial grade, and the other $1,000 on supplies. Tina took evening business classes for a year to figure out what went wrong the first time around before she dove into the relish business again. She determined that her parents had tried to expand too quickly with new, untested products and too small a financial cushion. So she took a more conservative approach. She based her business out of her home for several years and didn't hire full-time workers until she had enough in reserve to pay their salaries for six months without extra revenue coming in. Her gourmet chutneys are now on shelves regionally. Tina employs five people and plans to go national with her product someday. Her recipes came from her family's failed business.

"I started slow because I didn't want to lose my shirt, but working from home also allowed me to keep in better touch with my children," Tina says.

In addition to taking classes, budding entrepreneurs should talk to potential customers and suppliers. Take an informal survey and find out if suppliers would be interested in selling your product, how much they'd pay for it, and if there are any competitors. Once you find out who your competitors are, call the ones you're not competing with directly. Ask them about the pitfalls and nuances of the business. Offer to pay them for their time as consultants. Some will take you up on it; others will be glad to share their knowledge for free because finally they've found someone as passionate about their profession as they are.

Another good source is trade associations. They usually have conducted research on the industry and have directories of companies that you may be competing against. Consult the *Gale Encyclopedia of Business and Professional Associations*, the *Small Business Sourcebook*, and *Business Information Sources*.

You also need to figure out how many potential customers there are in your area and in the country at large. Consult your local economic development authority, possibly the chamber of commerce, which usually has information on population trends, payroll statistics, and income characteristics like utilities. Also, contact the U.S. Census Bureau for the latest national figures and county agencies that track population density and distribution tracts, showing the number of people living in specific areas such as precincts, water districts, and neighborhoods.

FINANCING

One of the biggest complaints of female entrepreneurs is that they didn't have enough capital. It's important to take your time and investigate all the angles.

During the planning stage, you should consult an accountant familiar with small business issues and your industry in particular. Ask her to figure out when it's realistic to expect you'll generate income, since you might be overly optimistic. Once you figure out how much money you'll need, you can start raising it.

Most money for small businesses is raised from friends and family. Be careful and only borrow from people you know can afford to lose it and are relaxed about it. You don't need a complaining investor on top of everything else you're taking on. Acquaintances rather than friends might be an even better way to go. Ask your accountant and attorney if they know of any clients looking for an investment.

Laura, the children's video entrepreneur, read books and put together a business plan. Then she approached friends and family about making an investment in her business. She made a point to only ask people to invest who wouldn't be devastated if they lost the money. She wouldn't accept money from her parents because she didn't want to tamper with their retirement money. She took friends to lunch and made her pitch. If they showed interest, she gave them the business plan. She raised the money but now regrets the decision to go to outside investors.

"I think I gave away too much of the company for too little money. I was afraid of using my own money, and I wish I did. I'd say to anyone else starting a business, 'Don't be afraid to use your own money,'" Laura says.

To keep costs down, Laura bartered for services and called in every favor she could. She signed up to be in a toy fair. She borrowed furniture for the booth. She asked a printer friend for a favor and got a reduced rate for postcards, which she handed out at the fair.

"Not knowing everything about the industry you start a business in can work to your advantage because you do things differently. I figured out how to do things cheaper and didn't follow traditional rules," Laura says.

She estimates that the videos generate about $100,000 in revenue annually and she's close to paying back the investment made in the company.

The biggest thing she's learned: don't rely on your friends to buy your product. Laura thought she could count on friends and relatives to buy a couple hundred video tapes but many friends and some family assumed they'd get the videos for free or as gifts.

"They don't think of supporting you in that way. They assume you'll make it with or without their help so it doesn't matter," Laura says.

The U.S. Office of Economic Development provides financing and information on finding other sources of capital. If your town has high unemployment or low per capita income you may be eligible for a loan because the state is encouraging businesses in your area.

So-called angels and venture capitalists usually want a large percentage of the company in exchange for their money and demand to see evidence of quick and sustained growth in the business plan. These are usually better options for businesses that are established but want to grow. Angels are people who invest in businesses looking for a higher return than they would see in traditional investments, typically provide $200,000 or less, and expect roughly 25 percent annual return on their investment. There are angel organizations that show your business plan to their investors and charge a fee for it. Fees can range from $25 to $2,000. On average they accept three deals for every ten reviewed.

Holly tried the angel investor route when she decided to open her own piroshki shop. The mother of three started making the Russian stuffed pastries when she was a little girl. Judging by everyone's response whenever she made them, she thought she had a quick growth business. Her friends inhaled the delicate layers of phyllo dough wrapped around beef, ham, or apple filling. But investors didn't think the business would soar.

"I had a very detailed business plan. I even cited profits made by piroshki shops in other cities, but they weren't interested in baked goods, they wanted high-tech plans," Holly says.

Though she's out the $100 she paid the angel organization to look at her plan, she doesn't feel the process was a waste.

"Making the presentation forced me to hone my pitch to the point that it became good and succinct. I ended up pitching the plan to local businessmen and two of them gave me money."

Holly went to friends and family for the rest of her needed capital. She didn't have enough to lease the store space she wanted, so she opened a small piroshki booth on the side of a heavily used commuter road. She operates the booth from 7:00 A.M. to 10:00 A.M. After six months of work, she has saved enough money to lease store space if she wants.

"Now I don't know if I want to open a store. I like the hours at the booth," she says.

You can consider borrowing against your stock or bond portfolio with a margin account. You'll have to pay interest but in some cases a portion of the interest could be tax deductible. It's a good idea to check with a tax advisor to see what applies. Margin accounts are risky. If the market goes against you, your broker can liquidate some or all of your portfolio without contacting you. You'll have no say as to which securities in your account will be sold. Some firms make "house calls," meaning they raise their margin requirements for certain volatile stocks when prices are fluctuating sharply and issue an immediate margin call. To maintain your position, don't borrow against more than 50 percent of your account or monitor the price of the stocks in your margin account daily and keep cash in a checking account so that you can promptly meet a margin call. The Securities and Exchange Commission offers an online calculator to help you estimate the likelihood of a margin call.

Grants are available for nonprofit companies. The *Federal Register*, published weekdays by the federal government, has grant announcements. You can look up the *Register* at the public library. The Small Business Innovation Research Award Program provides grants to technology-related businesses that address the needs of the government.

You could also consider a consumer bank loan. Some types of consumer loans are: second mortgage and home equity loans; uncollateralized personal loans; first mortgage refinance; and home equity lines of credit.

You can also sell assets. Not the most sexy sounding option, but a safe one. Consider selling your car and leasing one instead. Have a garage sale. You could even ask friends and family if they have junk they want to get rid of. They may give you the stuff without asking for money back because they're so happy to get rid of it, or they may ask for a cut.

You can even borrow against a whole life policy. If you've had your whole life policy for three years or more, you probably have some cash value in it. Many companies will let you borrow up to 90 percent of the value of your policy. As long as you continue to pay the premiums, your policy will remain intact. Loans against the cash value of your life insurance have interest, but less than if you take cash advances on your credit card.

Some women fund their companies with credit cards: a risky move that should only be considered by those with a financial safety net who are really good at accounting.

A couple of lawyers bartered their legal knowledge for in-kind services. Some got federal funding through the U.S. Small Business Administration. There are also programs like Count-Me-In for Women's Economic Independence, a loan system that is more female friendly than traditional banks.

Once you get your business running, another way to obtain money is factoring.

When you factor, you sell the money you are owed on receivables to a third party. The factor advances you between 50 and 90 percent of the value of your receivables and then collects the money from your creditors. When the full amount is collected, the factor gives you the remaining 10 to 50 percent, less fees. Fees are in the range of 1 to 5 percent of the amount financed. To find a factor look in the *Edwards Directory of American Factors* and contact the Commercial Finance Association.

Most women we talked to got creative and made do with much less than they thought they originally needed. They jerry-rigged secondhand furniture and tools or borrowed equipment, worked out of their homes, recruited friends to work for free, and funded their businesses out of operating income. If you're a one-woman operation working from home, your overhead is low. You can make more mistakes and recover quicker than if you have a payroll to make.

Others got free advice at local entrepreneurial training programs, which are often geared toward women. Many women entrepreneurs say that there is a willingness in the female community to share financing secrets.

"Most of us don't see one another as a threat," says Jennifer, owner of Naissance. "I've been there. You're starting out and you don't know if your idea is crazy, if you'll fail."

GETTING STARTED

All the mothers we talked to said think cheap, low overhead, so that if it doesn't work you can cut your losses quickly. Another mantra is subcontract: You want to contract out all the work you can't do yourself until you can predict your income flow because having to come up with payroll would be stressful. You should think conservatively until you can pay yourself a salary. You might not think you have a lot of extra brainpower after dealing with children all day, but you'd be amazed at how much room there is for trying to do something you love and how resourceful you can be.

Anne Marie, a former saleswoman for a software firm, launched her organic dog treat business as an act of remembrance for her dog. She spent $3,000 for the first three months of operation. She enlisted her sister, an artist, to help design the logo. She snagged her husband to put together a Web site and enlisted her stepdad to write a tribute to her dog to put on the Web site. She joined a nonprofit group for free market research. She hired a neighbor to help her bake the biscuits in preparation for New Hampshire's largest product expo, which put Rodz Pawz on the radar of stores.

The biscuits were an invention of necessity when her beloved dog, Rodney, developed skin rashes so horrible that at one point she covered the dog in salve and put her husband's underwear on Rodney to keep him from scratching.

"It was so traumatic. We spent thousands of dollars on tests for thyroid disorders and autoimmune diseases. We finally found out he was allergic to preservatives and beef by-products in dog food," Anne Marie said.

So that's when she developed her own dog biscuit. She did research on ingredients on the Internet from 9:00 P.M. when her kids went to bed to 2:00 A.M. She averaged about four hours of sleep a night for three months.

She found that garlic has good medicinal properties, oats are good for digestion and provide potassium and niacin, soy flour provides protein, and milk provides calcium. The mixture also tasted good to Rodney. Her dog loved her biscuits.

He died a couple of years ago. Anne Marie grieved for months, then realized she should do something with her recipe in honor of Rodney.

"I was home with the kids and I felt the need to do something else. I had developed this recipe so I decided to see if I could do something with it," she says.

She approached the New Hampshire Society for the Prevention of Cruelty to Animals and told them she was donating several bags of biscuits to the group. They could sell them and keep the profits. The only thing she asked for in return was feedback on the biscuits.

"Several people have approached the society with requests to sell biscuits through them and they usually say no but they told me they said yes to me because I was offering them for free and because of my enthusiasm," she says.

The experience was invaluable. Anne Marie got feedback on her labels and on problems with the biscuits. They got moldy after two weeks and they were too big for smaller dogs. It was free market research.

So Anne Marie went back to the drawing board. She tried to cook the biscuits longer. They burned. She got a convection oven, the kind that promotes airflow around the whole biscuit. The oven didn't work. She looked into all-natural preservatives like vitamins C and E, but they're not easy for some dogs to digest, so she checked them off her list.

The solution came to her by accident. She left biscuits in her sunroom one bright day and the sun took enough moisture out of the biscuits to preserve them.

"It shows that the solutions to problems aren't always the most expensive or complicated," Anne Marie says.

Jackie launched her skin and body care line over her kitchen stove in between warming bottles for her twins.

"It started out as Christmas presents for my family. I became obsessed with making the right blend. It gave me something else to focus on besides lack of sleep and cranky babies," Jackie said. "Once I was done making the Christmas gifts, I missed creating the lotions. I decided to make it into a business. I didn't have a lot of money so I had to think conservatively."

She mixed ingredients until she perfected three recipes, contracted a chemist to help her stabilize the formulas (using money loaned to her by her parents), and then subcontracted a manufacturer. She ordered small batches in bottles of only one size to make handling inventory easier. She sold small amounts, usually ten bottles of each of the three types of lotion, to local shops.

She personally checked her stock in each store daily. On a weekly basis, she straightened and changed the look of the displays. She brought in different colors of fabric to put under the lotions and containers to hold them. She kept meticulous notes on which products sold well with what display.

"I was incredibly hands-on the first few years. I constantly fiddled with the in-store displays until I figured out the best presentation. I got to know the shop owners really well. They'd tell me what kinds of things their customers were asking for. It was a cheap form of market research," Jackie said.

Sometimes the stores let her collect the money she earned on a daily basis. She used her earnings to fund her production.

PUBLIC RELATIONS

One investment Jennifer, owner of Naissance, recommends making early on is paying a good public relations firm to help you get your company's name out there.

TIPS ON HOW TO FIND A GOOD PR FIRM

- Figure out what your goals are. What do you want a public relations firm to do for you?
- Ask business people you trust for recommendations on agencies they've used.
- Check out the Public Relations Society of America Web site, www.prsa.org, for local agencies.
- Get five names. Call and ask about their experience in your field and for customer references.
- Review the information and pick three agencies to meet with.
- In the interviews, see if you're compatible with the people who would manage your account and if they know the industry. Use some buzzwords and see if they know them.
- Get a proposal from all three, which should include their understanding of your problem, strategies to tackle it, a timetable and budget.
- Once you have all three proposals you can evaluate and negotiate the price range. Costs can vary from a few hundred to a few thousand dollars.
- Negotiate a payment plan that you're comfortable with and that has regular monthly charges.
- Inform the two agencies you didn't choose about your decision.

The firm Jennifer hired got Naissance a blurb about its thermal T-shirts on a popular Web site, Daily Candy. As a result, the store sold out of its three hundred shirts.

"A good PR firm helps you brand your company and allows you to get your message out there," Jennifer says.

The store's sales have skyrocketed since it opened six years ago. Jennifer Aniston wore its designs when her character was pregnant on *Friends* and other celebrities are constantly outfitted in Naissance clothes for real pregnancies, thanks to word of mouth, connections to the right stylists, and well-placed articles.

"People told me my designs were too sexy and too young but I trusted my own instinct and it's worked out. That's the biggest thing I would tell people—to trust themselves."

The one time Jennifer didn't trust her own judgment she regretted it. She wanted to do a catalog of her line of clothing, so she hired a catalog consultant to put it together. He recommended that Jennifer hire an expensive photographer, rent ware-

---

THINGS TO THINK ABOUT WHEN SETTING UP YOUR OWN BUSINESS

- Write down the steps involved in creating your product or providing your service from start to finish.
- At each step write down the things needed to make the product and list the costs involved with each aspect.
- Study this list and try to find creative ways to cut costs, for example, can you barter? Get some things at cost? Make smaller batches?
- Talk to other people in the industry but who aren't direct competition. Get their advice.

house space, and load up on inventory. Every bit of the advice was wrong.

"We could've used a cheaper photographer, not rented the warehouse, and used the inventory in the store. We spent a lot more than we needed to and carried more inventory than I feel comfortable with," Jennifer says.

But she says mistakes are a good thing as long as you learn from them.

"Fear is good too. It's a driving factor in starting a business. You have to be a risk taker," she says. "When I first started people kept asking me if I had a pro forma. I still don't know exactly what a pro forma is."

WORKING YOUR OWN HOURS

A huge advantage to working for yourself is setting your own hours. You can get to the kids' soccer games and school plays and still work later that night.

That's what Stacy thought when she started her own photography studio out of her house. She has gained quite a following with the families in her city for taking natural photos of children, the kind of pictures that look like they could almost be really good snapshots.

But the adjustment to at-home work after being in an office is challenging for some. Stacy says the first few months were lonely. Sure, she had her three children to keep her company, but she missed talking to people who could utter more than one syllable and she missed talking to people about the marketing industry.

"You feel like you're under house arrest at first," she says.

The ability to work whenever and as much as she wanted was

also a difficult adjustment. In the beginning, Stacy says she didn't manage her time well. Tasks that normally took her an hour to complete would stretch over two or three hours at home. She'd have the television on or she'd get distracted by cleaning the house or entertaining one of her children halfway through the task.

"You have to establish clear boundaries around your work. Now I go into my darkroom and close the door when my youngest daughter takes a nap, and I use a part-time nanny to help care for the kids. But my arrangement isn't perfect," she said. "Sometimes my daughter wakes up when I'm in the darkroom."

If the nanny isn't there when that happens, Stacy usually tells her daughter to go to her playroom and she'll be there in a minute. She finishes up the photos that are developing and quits for the day.

When she schedules a photo shoot she makes sure the nanny is there to look after her children, though their noisy play can be distracting at times.

"My clients understand I have a small children at home. I think that fact helps put the children at ease during the photo shoots."

And yet, even with all the adjustments, Stacy wouldn't trade her new job for anything.

"I'm really big on the flexibility and freedom of it. Sometimes I work on the weekends. Sometimes I work after five," she says.

Stacy has even developed her product line further. She has started making DVDs that incorporate old super 8 film footage, photos, video, and new footage.

Most women report working harder for themselves than they did when someone else employed them, which means working late at night and early in the morning. When you work for yourself, it doesn't feel like just a job, it's who you are. Many think the success or failure of their venture is a direct reflection of their identity, so they do backflips to make things work. Remember, it's okay to fail, work part time, or take a day off. But here's the rub—working with your child nearby is great as long as she's quiet or a nanny is around. Be prepared to add more child-care hours, even if you're working from home. Two-year-olds aren't great with "just a minute," or "not now."

Jennifer knows about hard work. She regularly works twelve-hour days, sometimes more. She still stays late into the night to stock new inventory.

"At least one woman a day comes into the store and says, 'You have the ideal life. I'd love to have my own store.' But I don't think they know what goes into running a business. It's not putting a cute T-shirt on a woman and hanging around talking."

TRANSITIONING TO WORKING YOUR OWN HOURS

- Set a schedule for yourself and stick to it.
- Set specific and achievable goals on productivity and/or client development, for example, you will call two potential clients a day.
- During the times you're working make sure you have child care, at least for the first few weeks.
- Join professional organizations to get your fix of adult conversation. You can attend meetings and do online chats.
- Dress for work. It may help put you in the right mindset at first.
- Don't be too hard on yourself. Recognize this is a change that will take some time to adapt to.

Jennifer has a nanny. She makes a point to have breakfast with her two sons and drive them to school.

"They understand I'm working and I think it's a good role model," she says.

Jennifer has become addicted to the entrepreneurial buzz. She's in the middle of opening a chain of nail salons called Varnish. The idea is to have a mid-priced product with uniform guidelines, including sterilized instruments and consistent time spans for procedures. The salon has cork walls and Jetson-sleek furniture.

Her passion still lies in maternity wear, however, and she'd like to license her designs overseas in the next couple years.

"You have to go for it," she says.

RAMPING UP

Anne Marie plans to ramp up her Rodz Pawz dog biscuit business when her kids start school.

"When all the kids are in school, I'd like to land a national account," she said.

At the moment, she's content to develop contacts, work on her product, and supplement her family's income. She says there are positive things about launching the business on a smaller scale. She has the opportunity to work out the kinks, make mistakes early, and have a longer time to raise money for a big roll-out.

"When I introduce a new product, it's good to know the people I'm selling it to. I have a ready-made research group," Anne Marie said.

The research group came in handy when she created a doggy gift basket in the shape of a bone. She bought three hundred baskets, Frisbees, and T-shirts to put in the baskets. She thought the whole package would sell out quickly. It didn't. Within the first couple months she sold thirty.

She cut her losses, didn't order any more, or spend money on promoting it. She has two-hundred-odd baskets in her basement and pulls them out for charity auctions and Christmas gifts.

Tara wants to open her own clothing boutique in a few years when all three of her children are in school. Right now she's building up her retail experience. She rented a booth at an antiques market and sold vintage purses. The experience gave her a better idea of what price points customers felt comfortable with and what types of handbags would sell well without having to invest in huge overhead. She approached a couple other stores about taking clothes she designed as well as vintage items she reconstructed on consignment. They agreed. She has been able to further her knowledge of what sells well at what price as well as build a brand around her name.

Recently Tara took a part-time job at a small independently owned clothing store. She's honing her customer service skills and learning more about what kind of clothing mix she'll need to offer to compete with the big department stores.

"I look at this as a low-cost business degree," she said.

Maria designed and marketed a line of preteen girls' clothing from home, eventually converting her living and dining rooms into a mini-warehouse and shipping center. As her business grew, she enlisted the help of her four children. They earned allowance money labeling and tagging clothes and helping with packing and shipping. Her oldest daughter took orders over the phone and her two sons entertained themselves using the label gun.

"Every one of my children had a little part of the business and they enjoyed it," she said.

When Hayley, a former systems analyst, started her children's clothing business she decided to limit herself to tie-dyed clothes to keep the cost down. She also used her daughter and her daughter's friends as a test market. She invited them over after school and let them play dress up with the clothes, noting which ones they liked.

To keep costs down and her hours manageable, she decided to start selling the clothes through word of mouth and at home parties. She didn't want to invest in a retail space without a proven seller.

She's made her clothing for three years now and broke even this year. She's looking at several options for expanding the line, which she'll test out in the next year with her daughter and her friends. If they work, she says, they will pay for the rent on a retail location.

WAYS TO KEEP COSTS DOWN

- Get family members involved. If they have a skill, like Web site design, guilt them into providing it for free. Then when you make money you can reimburse them.
- Get a booth at a local craft or business fair. It's a low cost way to advertise your business.
- Keep your batches of products uniform. Perfect one product line before you move on to another. It's cheaper and easier to deal with logistically.
- Sell your product on consignment at other stores before you attempt to open your own. You can adjust the product and price point much easier this way.
- Always ask advice. Continually pick the brains of business people you admire. You'll get your best ideas that way.

MULTIPLE REVENUE STREAMS

Another thing to consider when starting your own business are the ancillary ways you can make money.

Sandy, the yoga studio owner, says she makes quite a bit of her money off of sales of bottled water, yoga mats, and T-shirts. Providing customers with simple impulse purchases can make the difference between profitability and losing money. Ever notice that in most Wal-Mart grocery aisles there are bananas? Know why? Because the company figured out that bananas are the number one impulse purchase of its customers.

Another way to increase revenue is to extend your brand. Jennifer, owner of the maternity store Naissance, started selling maternity clothes she designed wholesale to maternity stores across the country. The strategy increased her brand identity, made alliances with what others would perceive as competitors, and gave her inroads and valuable purchasing research regarding other markets if she chose to expand her store.

Danielle owns a public relations firm. She also teaches public relations at a local college, does voice-overs for commercials, and writes copy for commercials.

"I do so many things because then when one thing falls through, it's not the end of the world, there's always something else I can focus my energy on," she said.

Ana, the owner of Ana Brazil, a store selling Brazilian goods and food, employs dozens of revenue-generating techniques. She sells food as well as clothing and jewelry. She leases her store out after hours for business parties. She also provides fax services, prepaid calling cards, and money transfers for Brazilian expatriates.

FAILURE

Half of all new small businesses with employees fail in four years, according to the U.S. Small Business Administration. Two-thirds of those that fail will survive at least two years. The other third will fail before two years have elapsed. The number of small businesses without employees that survive after four years is significantly higher, but the SBA doesn't have exact numbers. That's good news: It means that if you take it slow, you have a better chance of success.

Emily failed at her first foray into catering. She underpriced her product and overextended herself—making too many promises to cater too many events. In two months she blew through the $2,000 she set aside to start the business. Six months into her foray she was in the red by $4,000. That's when she pulled the plug.

"It was crushing. I knew I made tasty food. I had plenty of customers but I didn't have the organization," Emily said.

After she closed her business, Emily took business courses and did market research. A year later, she tried again. This time she succeeded.

"I made that failure a case study. I looked at it from all the angles. I realized my mistakes and started over again," she said.

Emily upped the price of her food, hired part-time workers during the holidays, planned her time better, and figured out her niche. She noticed that family gatherings and reunions were on the rise. They wanted catered food because they didn't have the time to cook it themselves. But they didn't want just any catered food. When families get together they want comfort food with a twist. So instead of your regular macaroni and cheese, she whips up three-cheese macaroni with caramelized onions. She offers hickory smoked turkey or deep fried turkey with jalapeño cranberry stuffing at Thanksgiving.

"When people are around their mother and father, they get nostalgic for old flavors, but they've outgrown the Velveeta and white bread," she says.

Emily grossed $60,000 in the first six months of 2004.

"I've never experienced a failure as bad as my first business dying. I was depressed for weeks, but I came out of it okay and that's a good thing to learn—I can survive," she says.

Tiffany started a secretarial service from her home only to shut it down after seven months. Why? She wasn't ready to spend as much time away from her six- and eight-year-old boys as the business needed.

"I was in the same house with them but I was working fifty or sixty hours a week. I wasn't helping them with their homework, I didn't know how they were doing in school or what they were watching on television," she says.

Tiffany had a long list of clients and projects that needed to be completed. She made enough money to fund the family vacation and buy a new car in the seven months she worked.

"The money was nice. But I missed my boys. I'm not ready to work full time, even if it's from home."

Tiffany told her clients that she was shutting down the business, fulfilled the orders they had placed, and referred them elsewhere.

"I'd think about trying a business again in a couple of years. But the boys would have to be older and I'd have to limit my clients," she says.

Though the business didn't fit her schedule, she says it's nice to know that when she wants to go back to work, there's a market for her skills.

COMMON MISTAKES

Incorporating Too Quickly

The first step for many people when they launch a business is to file with the state office of incorporation. While incorporating is an appropriate step for many businesses, it pays to wait until your business idea is well formed before taking the plunge. The reason: The concept of your business, and therefore the name, is likely to change during the first few months of operation.

Not Researching the Market

A frequently overlooked component of business start-ups is determining whether there is a target market for your product or service. Arrange to speak to as many of your potential customers as possible. Questions should include: Would you buy my product or service? Where do you currently obtain this product or service? How much would you be willing to pay for it? What do you like /dislike about your current provider? Where would you look for this product or service when you need it?

Overusing an Attorney

Attorneys' hourly fees add up extremely quickly and their first few legal bills often shock newly minted business owners. The temptation is to involve your attorney in all aspects of your business for counsel and drafting of documents. Many business owners quickly learn that it pays to do your own research before contacting an attorney, draft documents for your attorney to use or use business document templates, and gather all information before meeting the first time. It'll save money if you do a lot of the legwork.

Spending Too Much Money on Office Space

A nice office and great computer equipment make many entrepreneurs feel as though their dream of entrepreneurism is coming true. While one of the pleasures of launching a business is setting up an office that you are proud of, expensive trappings have put many businesses out of business before they got off the ground.

Underestimating the Time the Business Will Take

When you start your own business, you work crazy long hours. Sometimes the women we talked to pulled eighty- or one-hundred-hour workweeks. This pace puts a huge strain on the family. The kids miss you. Your husband is exhausted because he's almost a single parent. Your babysitting bills skyrocket. Make sure you plot out your expected work hours before you start your business.

Starting your own business is tricky. A lot of people fail. Most entrepreneurs have a failed business under their belts before they hit on a success. They learned from their mistakes and did it differently the next time around. Don't be discouraged. There's always a next time.

A Final Note

Things are changing. It's inevitable. Decades ago, women fought for and won the right to equal treatment and opportunity in the workplace. Such a dramatic change in the social order of things was bound to spawn a few issues, kinks in the system to work out over time.

"The world is waking up to the importance of women staying home with the kids," one former stay-at-home mom who is now back in the workforce told us.

That's true. Experts are acknowledging the important role an available parent has in the development of a child. That doesn't mean that the hands of time are turning back on women in the workplace. The move toward real equality for women at work marches on.

Instead, it means that women will feel increasingly able to move freely between work and home without being professionally punished or made to feel inadequate in some way for doing so. Those of us who make these moves now will be leaders in a new women's movement—one that recognizes the value women have to offer both at work and at home.

Driving the success of this new women's movement is a basic unchanging truth: Men and women are different. It's a simple fact of life that must and should be finally accommodated in the workplace.

As one mom we talked to noted, "It's patently ridiculous to penalize women who have children. It's a fact of life."

Another told us, "It bothers me when women can't admit they're not the same as men. We just need to be ourselves."

So how can we be ourselves and feel successful in all aspects of our lives? One fifty-year-old former stay-at-home mom who now teaches at a university summed things up pretty well: "I think as a woman everything that you want in life you can accomplish. You just have to be patient. If you're patient, you really can have it all."

Resources

CHAPTER TWO. Feathering the Nest

"Raising a Child Calculator" can be found at www.babycenter.com.

Parents magazine, "Can I Afford to Quit?" www.parents.com/quiz/quitjob_0405.jsp.

"How Much Am I Spending?" calculator is located at www.chooseto save.org.

Books for Vetting Baby Gear

Consumer Reports, *Consumer Reports Best Baby Products*, 8th ed. (Consumer Reports, 2004). Yonkers, NY.

Denise Fields and Alan Fields, *Baby Bargains: Secrets to Saving 20 Percent to 50 Percent on Baby Furniture, Equipment, Clothes, Toys, Maternity Wear, and Much, Much More!*, 6th ed. (Windsor Peak Press, 2005). Boulder, CO.

Vicki Iovine and Peg Rosen, *The Girlfriend's Guide to Baby Gear* (Perigee Trade, 2003). New York, NY.

Information on Zipcar is at www.zipcar.com.

Insurance information can be found at www.insure.com.

A comparison of health benefits and medical insurers is found at www.planforyourhealth.com.

Bargains can be found at www.cairo.com and www.froogle.com.

Cookbooks

American Heart Association, *American Heart Association Quick & Easy Cookbook: More than 200 Healthful Recipes You Can Make in Minutes* (Clarkson Potter, 2001). New York, NY.

Betty Crocker, *Betty Crocker 4-Ingredient Dinners* (Wiley Publishing Inc., 2003). New York, NY.

Phyllis Pellman Good, *Fix-It and Forget-It Lightly: Healthy Low-Fat Recipes for Your Slow Cooker* (Good Books Publishing, 2004). Intercourse, PA.

Cynthia Stevens Graubart and Catherine Fliegel, *The One-Armed Cook: Quick and Easy Recipes, Smart Meal Plans, and Savvy Advice for New (and Not-So-New) Moms* (Meredith Books, 2005) Des Moines, IA.

Mable Hoffman, *Mable Hoffman's Crockery Cookery, Revised Edition* (HP Trade, 1995). New York, NY.

Dawn J. Ranck, *Fix-It and Forget-It Cookbook: Feasting with Your Slow Cooker* (Good Books Publishing, 2001). Intercourse, PA.

CHAPTER THREE. Departure Strategies

Equal Employment Opportunity Commission (EEOC), www.eeoc.gov.

Pregnancy Discrimination Act of 1978 in Title VII of the Civil Rights Act of 1964. For more information on provisions of the Act, see www .eeoc.gov/facts/fs-preg.html.

CHAPTER FIVE. Backlash

Stores with Outlets

Neiman Marcus, www.neimanmarcus.com.

Saks Fifth Avenue, www.saks.com.

Nordstrom, www.nordstrom.com.

Talbots, www.talbots.com.

Ann Taylor, www.anntaylor.com.

To find out more about the Junior League, visit their Web site at www.ajli.org.

CHAPTER SIX. One Foot In, One Foot Out

Volunteer Resources

Hands On Network, www.handsonnetwork.org.

Volunteer Match, www.volunteermatch.org.

Points of Light Foundation, www.pointsoflight.org.

Jenny Friedman, *The Busy Family's Guide to Volunteering: Doing Good Together* (Robins Lane Press, 2003) Beltsville, MD.

Michael Landes, *The Back Door Guide to Short-Term Job Adventures:*

Internships, Extraordinary Experiences, Seasonal Jobs, Volunteering, Working Abroad, 4th ed. (Ten Speed Press, 2005). Berkeley, CA.

John Raynolds, *Volunteering: How Service Enriches Your Life—and How Its Unexpected Halo Effect Boosts Your Career* (St. Martin's Press, 1999). New York, NY.

Athletic Resources

For information on beginning bicycle tours just for women, go to Luna Tours at www.lunatours.com.

To learn more about what's going on in female sports across the country, go to the American Alliance for Health, Physical Education and Dance Web site at www.aahperd.org.

To find out about running groups or to learn how to plan a race, see the American Running Association's Web site at www.americanrunning.org.

CHAPTER SEVEN. Part Time

For help in updating your résumé and interview skills, check out Women@Work Network at www.womenatworknetwork.com.

The following Web sites help stay-at-home moms find paid work:

www.jobsformoms.com

www.jobsandmoms.com

Read *Creating a Flexible Workplace: How to Select and Manage Alternative Work Options*, 2nd ed., by Barney Olmstead and Suzanne Smith (Amacom Books, 1994).

Job openings can be found at www.monster.com.

Work Support Groups

Flex-Time Lawyers, www.flextimelawyers.com.

Part-time Moms, www.mom-in-the-middle.com.

National Association of Part-time and Temporary Employees, www
.members.tripod.com/~NAPTE/.

Association of Part-time Librarians, www2.canisius.edu/~huberman/
aptl.html.

CHAPTER EIGHT. Going Back

For Information on au pairs, see the U.S. Department of State Web site,
www.state.gov.

CHAPTER NINE. Career Counseling

Working Mothers magazine publishes an annual 100 Best Companies list.

Vocation Vacations is a Portland, Oregon, company that introduces new
career fields for you to try. Learn more at www.vocationvacations.com.

The *Occupational Outlook Handbook* from the U.S. Labor Department's
Bureau of Labor Statistics (www.bls.gov/oco/home.htm) is a great resource for exploring possible new fields.

Internship Resources

Internships 2005 (Peterson's Internships), 25th ed. (Peterson's Guides,
2004). Lawrenceville, NJ.

The Internship Bible, 10th ed. (Random House, 2005). New York, NY.

Apprenticeship Resources

U.S. Department of Labor Employment and Training Administration, www.doleta.gov.

U.S. Chamber of Commerce, 1615 H Street NW, Washington, D.C. 20062-2000, (202) 659-6000, www.uschamber.com.

Wider Opportunities for Women, www.work4women.org.

Home Builders Institute, www.hbi.org.

National Joint Apprenticeship and Training Committee, www.njatc.org.

National Brotherhood of Electrical Workers, www.ibew.org.

CHAPTER TEN. Entrepreneurs

Have a great invention but don't know how to patent and produce it? Look at the Inventors Resources tab at www.tabletopper.com.

Lorna M. Daniells, *Business Information Sources*, 3rd ed. (University of California Press, 1993).

Robert E. Fleury, *The Small Business Sourcebook*, 3rd rev. ed. (Sourcebooks, 1996).

Michael B. Hullmantel, ed., *Gale Encyclopedia of Business and Professional Associations: A Guide to More Than 8,000 Business, Professional, Trade and Related Organizations* (Gale Group, 1995). Detroit, MI.

U.S. Census Bureau, www.census.gov.

Securities and Exchange Commission, 100 F Street, NE, Washington, D.C. 20549, (202) 551-6551, www.sec.gov.

U.S. Small Business Administration, www.sba.gov.

Small Business Innovation Research Award Program, www.sba.gov/sbir/indexsbir-sttr.html.

Count-Me-In for Women's Economic Independence, www.count-me-in.org.

Commercial Finance Association, 225 West Thirty-fourth Street, Suite 1815, New York, NY 10122, (212) 594-3490, www.cfa.com.

Public Relations Society of America, 33 Maiden Lane, 11th floor, New York, NY 10038-5150, www.prsa.org.

Index